FOREST TREES OF THE UNITED STATES AND CANADA
and How to Identify Them

FOREST TREES OF THE UNITED STATES AND CANADA

and How to Identify Them

ELBERT L. LITTLE, JR.

Chief Dendrologist (Retired)
Timber Management Research
Forest Service
United States Department of Agriculture

Dover Publications Inc.
New York

Published in Canada by General Publishing Company,
Ltd., 30 Lesmill Road, Don Mills, Toronto, Ontario.

Published in the United Kingdom by Constable and
Company, Ltd., 10 Orange Street, London WC2H 7EG.

This Dover edition, first published in 1979, is an un-
abridged and unaltered republication of the work orig-
inally published in 1978 by the Forest Service, United
States Department of Agriculture, Washington, D.C., as
Agriculture Handbook No. 519, entitled *Important
Forest Trees of the United States.*

International Standard Book Number: 0-486-23902-0
Library of Congress Catalog Card Number: 79-52527

Manufactured in the United States of America
Dover Publications, Inc.
180 Varick Street
New York, N.Y. 10014

CONTENTS

FOREST TREES OF THE UNITED STATES AND CANADA

and How to Identify Them

ELBERT L. LITTLE, JR.[1]

INTRODUCTION

An introduction to the forest trees of the United States is the object of this handbook. It aims to provide a popular, illustrated, compact reference for identifying important and common trees in the forests. Drawings, descriptions, and keys serve for identification, to find the name of a tree or specimen. Maps show where each species is native or grows wild. Principal uses and other notes are compiled, and State trees are listed.

This publication is based on an article with the same title published in "Trees, the 1949 Yearbook of Agriculture".[2] As Yearbook Separate 2156, that article has been reprinted several times and has been widely circulated through the years.

Colleagues in the Forest Service throughout the United States kindly have reviewed the original yearbook article. They have suggested improvements, and offered corrections, revisions, and additional data. Their assistance is greatly appreciated.

For a selected list of 204 species the following information is compiled here: (1) Approved common and scientific names, as well as other names in use; (2) drawings, keys, and brief, nontechnical descriptive notes for identification; (3) distribution maps and notes showing ranges; and (4) lists of principal uses, chiefly of the wood.

Several new features are included in this handbook, based upon additional material assembled during the interval of more than a quarter century. First, the total number of tree species has been enlarged from 165 to 204. The earlier publication was limited to continental United States including Alaska (the 49th State). Twelve trees from Hawaii (the 50th State) and 12 from the Commonwealth of Puerto Rico and the Territory of the Virgin Islands have been added as representatives of the rich tropical floras. Minor changes in common and scientific names have been adopted to conform to the latest Forest Service checklist (Little 1978).[3]

New maps have been drafted, based upon the detailed large ones in "Atlas of United States Trees" (Little 1971). Principal uses have been brought up to date, mainly from the new series on American Woods (Plank 1971). Information on State trees has been revised and expanded (USDA, Forest Service 1972). Also, measurements are given in the metric system as well as in feet and inches. A ruler with equivalents has been added on the last page.

[1] Chief dendrologist (retired), Timber Management Research, Forest Service, United States Department of Agriculture, Washington, D.C. 20250.

[2] Little, Elbert L., Jr. To know the trees: Important forest trees of the United States. In Trees, U.S. Dep. Agric., Yearb. Agric. 1949, p. 763–814, 909, illus. (maps). 1949.

[3] Names and dates in parentheses refer to Selected References, page 64.

Numbers of Tree Species

This handbook describes and illustrates about one-fourth of the native tree species of continental United States or, nearly one-third, if the tropical and subtropical species of southern Florida (almost 100) and the hawthorns (*Crataegus,* about 35 under a conservative treatment) are omitted. The total includes small trees not of commercial timber size as well as large shrubs that sometimes exceed minimum commercial timber sizes. Varieties and hybrids are not counted.

A definition may be appropriate, because the figures vary according to size limits. Trees may be defined as woody plants having one erect perennial stem or trunk at least 3 inches (7.5 cm) in diameter at breast height (4½ feet or 1.3 m), a more or less definitely formed crown of foliage, and a height of at least 13 feet (4 m). Though the division between trees and shrubs is not sharp, shrubs typically are the smaller woody plants, usually with several perennial stems branching from the base.

The native trees of continental United States, with numbers in parentheses for those trees described and illustrated in this handbook, total about 685 (180) species, according to the revised Forest Service checklist (Little 1978). These are grouped further into 218 (63) genera and 73 (32) plant families.

The largest genera, or groups, of native trees in continental United States with approximate numbers of species are: oaks (*Quercus*), 58 (30) species, hawthorn (*Crataegus*), about 35 (0); pines (*Pinus*), 36 (24); and willow (*Salix;* also shrubs), 27 (2).

The 204 species of forest trees of this handbook have been selected primarily for the commercial importance of their woods and other products. Several have other values in forestry. Some are common or dominant species in forest types over large areas.

Many other species from foreign lands have been introduced as ornamental, shade, and fruit trees. About 75 species of these widely planted foreign trees have escaped from cultivation and have become naturalized. They may be considered properly at home here, and a few have become weeds. More than 25 of these exotics are tropical trees confined to Florida. Introduced trees are outside the scope of this handbook but are included in Forest Service checklists. They are treated in publications about cultivated trees; for example, "Sixty Trees from Foreign Lands" (Little 1962).

Arrangement of Species and Descriptions

The 180 important forest tree species of continental United States have been arranged in two lists, eastern and western, because the trees of the two regions are almost entirely different. Eastern, the first list, contains 120 species, Nos. 1–120, found in the eastern half of continental United States, west to the prairie-plains. Western, the second list, has 60 species, Nos. 121–180, native in the western half of continental United States, west of the prairie-plains and including Alaska.

The eastern list is twice the size of the western. Eastern forests are mostly of deciduous or broadleaf trees and contain many species of commercial hardwoods. In contrast, the western forests are mainly of conifers and have fewer species. Several species of wide distribution in both East and West have been placed in the list with greater range, with cross-references.

The Hawaiian Islands, represented by Nos. 181–192, have about 300 to 370 species of native tropical

2

trees, nearly all found nowhere else. Puerto Rico and the Virgin Islands have more than 550 species of native tropical trees, from which Nos. 193–204 have been selected.

The 17 species of important forest trees of Alaska included here represent about half of the 49th State's 32 tree species and 6 shrub species sometimes attaining tree size. These Alaska species are listed by number on page 4 and are mentioned in the distribution notes.

Likewise, the important forest trees of Canada may be found in this handbook. The 90 Canadian species treated here are more than half the native trees of that country. (Several extend northward only to extreme southern Ontario, however.) These species are indicated in the maps and by mention of Canada or a Province in the notes.

Each species is numbered and has a short description. Size is indicated as large (more than 70 ft or 21 m tall), medium-sized (30–70 ft or 9–21 m tall), or small (less than 30 ft or 9 m tall). This grouping refers to average heights of mature trees on good sites. Of course, there are many exceptions.

The descriptive notes are a summary of the leading characteristics, such as bark, leaves, fruits, and also flowers if they are showy or distinctive. To aid identification, small drawings of leaves and fruit were made for the article in the 1949 Yearbook of Agriculture by Leta Hughey. Additions are by Barbara H. Honkala. Scale of reduction from natural size is indicated by fractions.

The distribution maps show concisely the geographic areas in contiguous United States and adjacent Canada and Mexico where each species grows wild, or is native. These maps have been reduced from the large ones in "Atlas of United States Trees," nearly all in Volume 1 (Little 1971). That reference may be examined for greater detail and for ranges beyond in Alaska and Canada. Volume 2 (Viereck and Little 1975) has large maps for Alaska.

Identification

Many trees can be identified directly from the drawings and maps. If names are known, further information can be located by the species numbers listed in the indexes (pages 66, 69). Then a check can be made by comparison with illustrations and descriptions.

Maps aid identification by showing which of several related tree species are native in a particular region and which are not to be expected. However, many species have been introduced beyond their mapped native ranges and are planted, escaped from cultivation, or naturalized as though wild.

To assist in the identification of trees in this handbook, a simple key, based chiefly upon leaves and twigs, has been inserted in the text. This key is an outline in which trees with certain characteristics in common are grouped together. Some notes in the key have not been repeated in the species descriptions.

With the key, the name of a tree is found by elimination; that is, through successive selection of one from a pair of lines whose descriptive characters agree with the specimen. The paired lines are designated by the same letter, single and double, beginning with "A" and "AA," at the left of the page. Under the line fitting the specimen, the elimination continues with the next pair indented below to the right, such as from "AA" to "N" or "NN" and from "NN" to "O" or "OO," etc., until the name is reached.

The arrangement of species in the lists of eastern and western trees is artificial, to fit the key, rather than botanical. In each list the conifers are placed first, sorted into those with needlelike leaves and those with scalelike leaves, followed by broadleaf trees. The latter are grouped into trees with paired (opposite) simple leaves, trees with paired (opposite) compound leaves, trees with single (alternate) compound leaves, and trees with single (alternate) simple leaves, with the oaks placed last. (A simple leaf has 1 blade. A compound leaf has 3 or more, usually smaller, blades or leaflets. Leaflets spread flattened in a plane on a leafstalk that sheds with them. Also, a leaf usually has a developing bud at its base, while leaflets do not.)

Additional information, especially about less common trees not found here, is available in various handbooks, tree guides, and similar publications (see Selected References, page 64). Other references for identification of trees and shrubs, including titles for each State and for cultivated species, are listed in a separate bibliography (Little and Honkala 1976). Information about publications on the trees of each State and how to obtain them may be available from the State Forester.

Trees are described also in the various botanical floras and manuals, usually technical and not illustrated, which have been prepared for geographical regions, States, and smaller areas. In further studies, some knowledge of botanical terms and systematic botany (plant taxonomy) or dendrology (tree identification) may be helpful.

If needed, assistance may be sought from specialists in plant identification. Plant taxonomists, or taxonomic botanists, are located in departments of botany and forestry of universities and colleges and in State agricultural experiment stations, botanical gardens, arboreta, herbaria, and museums.

Leafy twigs with flowers and fruits can be prepared for identification and further study. Similar botanical or herbarium specimens are mounted with labels and filed in large herbaria and museums. The samples are dried under pressure in a plant press, as are small flowers and leaves among the pages of a book.

A plant press consists of 2 frames, size about 12 by 18 in (30 by 45 cm), 2 straps, and blotters or driers. Specimens are placed within sheets of folded newspapers alternating with blotters, which are changed daily, dried in air or sun, and reused. In the absence of this equipment, specimens can be prepared under weights (such as books or bricks) by using other newspapers as blotters. Accompanying notes for label should include locality, date, size, whether wild or planted, uses and related information, any known common name, and collector's name with serial number.

ALASKA

The important forest trees of Alaska are included among these 17 species, which range northward from the lower 48 States through western Canada to the 49th: Nos. 2, 16, 17, 83, 88, 131, 134, 135, 136, 139, 142, 143, 150, 152, 164, 165, 168.

EASTERN

Tree species Nos. 1 to 120 are native wholly or mainly within the eastern half of continental or contiguous United States, west to the prairie-plains. Also, No. 164 from the western trees is partly eastern, No. 200 is native in the Southeast, and No. 197 in southern Florida. These tropical species are introduced in southern Florida, a few westward to California: Nos. 181, 183, 185, 188, 190, 194, 195, 196, 199, 201, 202.

1. Baldcypress.   2. Tamarack.   3. Eastern white pine.   4. Longleaf pine.

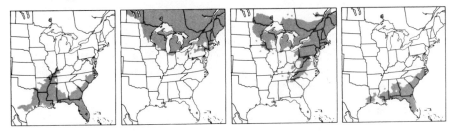

GYMNOSPERMS (CONIFERS OR SOFTWOODS)

A (AA on p. 11). Trees resinous, with leaves needlelike or scalelike, evergreen (except Nos. 1, 2); seeds borne on scales of a cone (berrylike in juniper, Nos. 23, 24)—**Gymnosperms** (conifers or softwoods, such as pines, spruces, firs).

  B. Leaves shedding in fall, on slender twigs mostly shedding in fall or leaves on short spur branches.

    C. Leaves needlelike or scalelike, on slender twigs mostly shedding in fall—**Baldcypress** (*Taxodium*).

1. Baldcypress, *Taxodium distichum* (L.) Rich. (southern-cypress, cypress, swamp-cypress, red-cypress, yellow-cypress, white-cypress, tidewater red-cypress, gulf-cypress). Variety: pond-cypress, var. *nutans* (Ait.) Sweet. Large tree with swollen base and "knees," swamps, ponds, and river banks, South Atlantic and Gulf Coastal Plains and Mississippi Valley. Bark reddish brown or gray, with long fibrous or scaly ridges. Leaves crowded featherlike in 2 rows on slender horizontal twigs, flat, ⅜–¾ in (1–2 cm) long (scalelike in pondcypress), light yellow green, or whitish beneath, shedding in fall. Cones ¾–1 in (2–2.5 cm) in diameter, of hard scales.

Principal uses: Chiefly building construction and heavy construction, including docks, warehouses, factories, and bridges. General millwork, boxes and crates, caskets and burial boxes, interior trim, and paneling. Tanks, vats, tubs, ships and boats, refrigerators, car construction, patterns, and flasks. The heartwood is well suited for siding because of its moderate decay resistance. Ornamental. (State tree of Louisiana.)

    CC. Leaves needlelike, many in cluster on short spur branches—**Larch** (or tamarack, *Larix*).

2. Tamarack, *Larix laricina* (Du Roi) K. Koch (eastern larch, American larch, Alaska larch, hackmatack). Medium-sized tree of wet soils in Northeastern United States, and across Canada to Alaska. Bark reddish brown, scaly. Needles many in cluster on short spur branches (or single on leading twigs), 3-angled, ¾–1 in (2–2½ cm) long, blue green, shedding in fall. Cones upright, ¾ in (2 cm) long.

Principal uses: Lumber (largely framing for houses). Railroad crossties and poles. Pulpwood.

  BB. Leaves evergreen, on normal twigs.

    D. Leaves needlelike, more than ½ in (12 mm) long (usually shorter in No. 17).

      E. Needles in clusters of 2–5 with sheath at base—**Pine** (*Pinus*).

        F. Needles 5 in cluster—**White (soft) pines.**

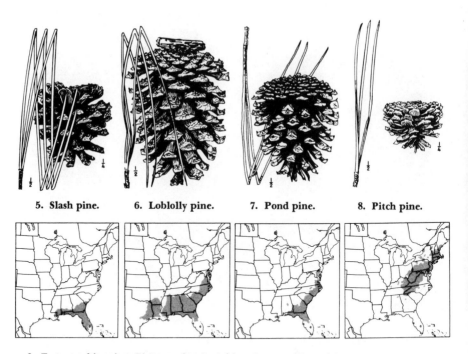

5. Slash pine. **6. Loblolly pine.** **7. Pond pine.** **8. Pitch pine.**

3. Eastern white pine, *Pinus strobus* L. (white pine, northern white pine, northern pine, soft pine, Weymouth pine). Large tree (largest northeastern conifer) of Northeastern United States, adjacent Canada, and Appalachian Mountain region; variety in mountains of Mexico and Guatemala. Bark gray or purplish, deeply fissured into broad ridges. Needles 5 in cluster, slender, 2½–5 in (6–13 cm) long, blue green. Cones long-stalked, long and narrow, 4–8 in (10–20 cm) long, yellow brown, with thin, rounded scales.

Principal uses: Construction, millwork, interior paneling, and trim. Pulpwood. Shade tree and ornamental. (State tree of Maine and Michigan. "Pine cone and tassel" is State flower of Maine.)

> FF. Needles 2 or 3 in a cluster—**Yellow (hard, or pitch) pines.**
>> G. Needles 3 in cluster.
>>> H. Needles mostly more than 8 in (20 cm) long.

4. Longleaf pine, *Pinus palustris* Mill. (longleaf yellow pine, southern yellow pine, long-straw pine, hill pine, pitch pine, hard pine, heart pine; *P. australis* Michx. f.). Large tree of South Atlantic and Gulf Coastal Plains. Bark orange brown, coarsely scaly. Needles 3 in cluster, slender, very long, 10–15 in (25–38 cm) long, dark green. Cones large, 5–10 in (13–25 cm) long, dull brown, prickly.

Principal uses: A leading world producer of naval stores. Lumber for miscellaneous factory and construction purposes, flooring, railroad-car construction, shipbuilding, poles and piling. Pulpwood.

5. Slash pine, *Pinus elliottii* Engelm. (yellow slash pine, swamp pine, pitch pine). Variety: South Florida slash pine, var. *densa* Little & Dorman. Large tree of South Atlantic and Gulf Coastal Plains. Bark purplish brown, with large thin scales. Needles 3 (or 2 and 3) in cluster, stout, 6–12 in (15–30 cm) long, dark green. Cones 3–6 in (7.5–15 cm) long, shiny brown, with minute prickles.

Principal uses: Same as No. 4.

>>> HH. Needles mostly less than 8 in (20 cm) long.

6. Loblolly pine, *Pinus taeda* L. (oldfield pine, North Carolina pine, shortleaf pine). Large tree of Atlantic and Gulf Coastal Plains. Bark reddish brown, deeply fissured into broad scaly plates. Needles 3 in cluster, slender, 6–9 in (15–23 cm) long, pale green. Cones 3–5 in (7.5–13 cm) long, reddish brown, with stiff, sharp prickles.

Principal uses: Important timber species. Same as No. 9. (Southern pine, *Pinus* spp., is the State tree of Alabama. Pine, *Pinus* spp., is the State tree of North Carolina.)

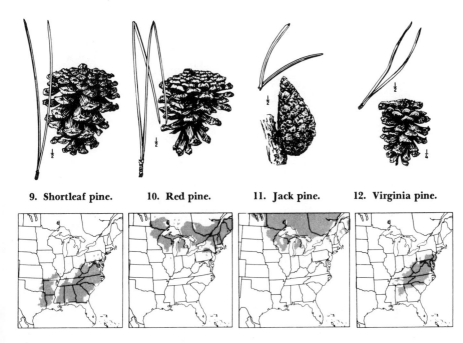

9. Shortleaf pine.　　**10. Red pine.**　　**11. Jack pine.**　　**12. Virginia pine.**

7. Pond pine, *Pinus serotina* Michx. (marsh pine, pocosin pine). Medium-sized to large tree of Coastal Plain of Southeastern United States. Bark dark reddish brown, furrowed into scaly plates. Needles 3 in cluster, slender, 6–8 in (15–20 cm) long, dark yellow green. Cones egg-shaped or rounded, 2–2½ in (5–6 cm) long, yellow brown, nearly stalkless, prickly, remaining closed and persistent.
Principal uses: Lumber. Pulpwood.

8. Pitch pine, *Pinus rigida* Mill. Medium-sized tree of Appalachian Mountain region and in adjacent Canada. Needles 3 in cluster, stout, 3–6 in (7.5–15 cm) long, dark yellow green. Cones short and broad, 1½–3 in (4–7.5 cm) long, light brown, shiny, with small prickles, remaining on branches several years after opening.
Principal uses: Lumber. Pulpwood.

> GG. Needles 2 in cluster (or partly 3 in No. 9).
>   I. Needles mostly more than 3 in (7.5 cm) long.

9. Shortleaf pine, *Pinus echinata* Mill. (shortleaf yellow pine, southern yellow pine, yellow pine, shortstraw pine, Arkansas pine). Large tree of southeastern quarter of United States north to New York. Bark reddish brown, with large, irregular, flat, scaly plates. Needles 2 or 3 in cluster, slender 2½–5 in (6–13 cm) long, dark blue green. Cones small, 1½–2½ in (4–6 cm) long, dull brown, with small prickles.
Principal uses: Important timber species. Lumber chiefly for building material including millwork, also plywood, boxes and crates, agricultural implements, motor vehicles, low-grade furniture. Veneer for containers. This and other southern pines are the leading native pulpwoods and leading woods in production of slack cooperage. Ornamental. (Pine, *Pinus* spp., is the State tree of Arkansas.)

10. Red pine, *Pinus resinosa* Ait. (Norway pine). Medium-sized to large tree of North-eastern United States and adjacent Canada. Bark reddish brown, with broad, flat, scaly plates. Needles 2 in cluster, slender, 5–6 in (13–15 cm) long, dark green. Cones 2 in. (5 cm) long, light brown, without prickles.
Principal uses: General building construction, planing-mill products, and general mill-work. Pulpwood. Ornamental and shade tree. (State tree of Minnesota.)

> II. Needles mostly less than 3 in (7.5 cm) long.

11. Jack pine, *Pinus banksiana* Lamb. (scrub pine, gray pine, black pine, Banksian pine). Usually small (or medium-sized) tree of Northeastern United States and eastern to north-western Canada. Bark dark brown, with narrow scaly ridges. Needles 2 in cluster, stout,

7

13. Sand pine. 14. Spruce pine. 15. Red spruce. 16. White spruce.

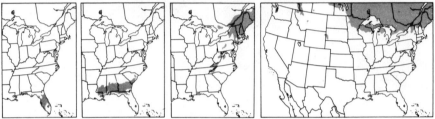

twisted, ¾–1½ in (2–4 cm) long, dark green. Cones 1-sided, much curved, small, 1–2 in (2.5–5 cm) long, light yellow, without prickles, remaining closed at maturity.
Principal uses: Pulpwood. Rough construction, boxes, crates, shipping containers, and prefabricated buildings. Ornamental.

12. Virginia pine, *Pinus virginiana* Mill. (scrub pine, Jersey pine). Usually small tree (sometimes large) of Atlantic Coastal Plain, Appalachian Mountain, and Ohio Valley regions. Bark dark brown, thin, with scaly plates. Needles 2 in cluster, stout, twisted, 2–3 in (5–7.5 cm) long, gray green. Cones 2 in (5 cm) long, reddish brown, shiny, very prickly.
Principal uses: Pulpwood. Lumber.

13. Sand pine, *Pinus clausa* (Chapm. ex Engelm.) Vasey ex Sarg. (scrub pine, spruce pine). Small to medium-sized tree confined to Florida and extreme South Alabama. Bark deeply furrowed into oblong reddish brown plates, on branches smooth gray. Needles 2 in cluster, slender, 2–3½ in (5–9 cm) long, dark green. Cones clustered, 2–3½ in (5–9 cm) long, brown, conical, turned back and nearly stalkless, prickly, mostly remaining closed and persistent.
Principal uses: Pulpwood. Lumber.

14. Spruce pine, *Pinus glabra* Walt. (cedar pine, bottom white pine). Medium-sized to large tree of Gulf and South Atlantic Coastal Plains. Bark on small trunks and limbs gray and smooth; bark on large trunks with flat scaly ridges. Needles 2 in cluster, slender, 1½–3 in (4–7.5 cm) long, dark green. Cones 1–2 in (2.5–5 cm) long, reddish brown, shiny, with minute prickles.
Principal uses: Lumber. Pulpwood.

    EE. Needles borne singly and not in clusters, without sheath at base.
      J. Twigs roughened by projecting bases of old needles; cones hanging down.
        K. Needles 4-angled, stiff, sharp-pointed, without leaf-stalk, extending out on all sides of twig—**Spruce** (*Picea*).

15. Red spruce, *Picea rubens* Sarg. (yellow spruce, West Virginia spruce, he-balsam; *P. rubra* (Du Roi) Link, not A. Dietr.). Medium-sized to large tree of Northeastern United States, adjacent Canada, and Appalachian Mountain region. Bark reddish brown, thin, scaly. Twigs hairy. Needles 4-angled, ½ in (12 mm) long, dark green, shiny. Cones 1¼–1½ in (3–4 cm) long, light reddish brown, shiny, with scales rigid, rounded, and often slightly toothed on edges.
Principal uses: Same as No. 16.

16. White spruce, *Picea glauca* (Moench) Voss (Canadian spruce, skunk spruce, cat

17. Black spruce. 18. Eastern hemlock. 19. Balsam fir. 20. Fraser fir.

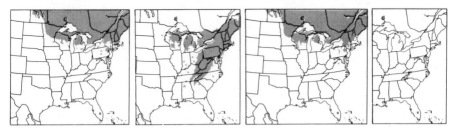

spruce, Black Hills spruce, western white spruce; *P. canadensis* (Mill.) B.S.P., not (Michx.) Link). Medium-sized tree of Northeastern United States, Black Hills, and across Canada to Alaska. Bark gray or brown, thin, scaly. Twigs hairless. Needles 4-angled, ½–¾ in (12–15 mm) long, blue green, of disagreeable odor when crushed. Cones slender, 1¼–2 in (3–5 cm) long, pale brown and shiny, with scales thin, flexible, rounded, and not toothed.

Principal uses: Pulpwood. Lumber for boxes and crates, construction, prefabricated dwellings, mobile homes, furniture, and pallets. Piano sounding boards, violins, and other musical instruments. Christmas trees. Ornamental and shade tree. Important timber species of Canada. (Black Hills spruce, var. *densata* Bailey, is the State tree of South Dakota.)

17. Black spruce, *Picea mariana* (Mill.) B.S.P. (bog spruce, swamp spruce). Small to medium-sized tree of bottom lands and bogs, Northeastern United States and across Canada to Alaska. Bark grayish brown, thin, scaly. Twigs hairy. Needles 4-angled, ¼–⅝ in (6–15 mm) long, pale blue green. Cones ⅝–1¼ in (1.5–3 cm) long, dull gray brown, with scales rigid, rounded, and slightly toothed.

Principal uses: Same as No. 16.

        KK. Needles flat, soft, blunt-pointed, with short leafstalk, appearing in 2 rows— **Hemlock** (*Tsuga*).

18. Eastern hemlock, *Tsuga canadensis* (L.) Carr. (Canada hemlock, hemlock spruce). Medium-sized to large tree of Northeastern United States, adjacent Canada, and Appalachian Mountain region. Bark brown or purplish, deeply furrowed into broad scaly ridges. Needles short-stalked, flat, soft, blunt-pointed, ⅜–⅝ in (10–15 mm) long, shiny dark green, lighter beneath, appearing in 2 rows. Cones ⅝–¾ in (1.5–2 cm) long, brownish.

Principal uses: Lumber for light framing, sheathing, roofing, and subflooring. Boxes, crates, and pallets: general millwork, signs, toys, and sporting goods. Pulpwood. Bark formerly was a source of tannin. Ornamental and shade tree. (State tree of Pennsylvania.)

        JJ. Twigs smooth; cones upright, in top of tree—**Fir** (*Abies*).

19. Balsam fir, *Abies balsamea* (L.) Mill. (balsam, Canada balsam, eastern fir). Medium-sized tree of Northeastern United States, Appalachian Mountain region, and across Canada to Alberta. Bark gray or brown, thin, smoothish, with many resin blisters, becoming scaly. Needles flat, ½–1¼ in (12–30 mm) long, dark green, usually rounded at tip. Cones upright, 2–3 in (5–7.5 cm) long, purple, with cone scales usually covering bracts.

Principal uses: A major pulpwood species. Lumber for light frame construction, interior knotty paneling, fish-box construction, crates, cooperage, millwork. Canada balsam (an oleoresin). Christmas trees and wreaths.

9

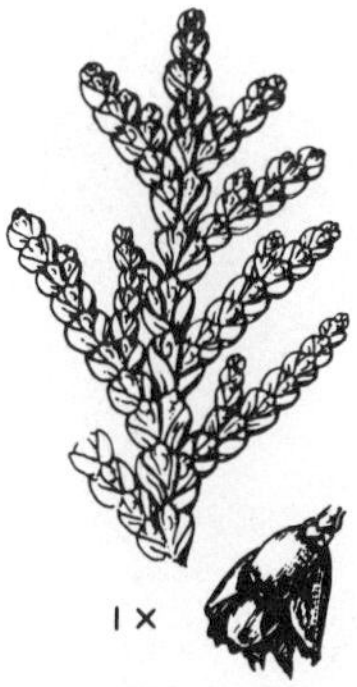

21. Northern white-cedar.

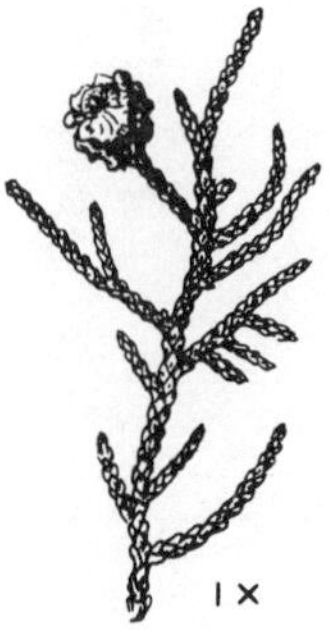

22. Atlantic white-cedar.

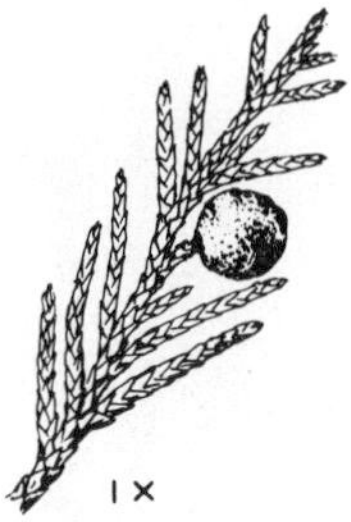

23. Eastern red-cedar.

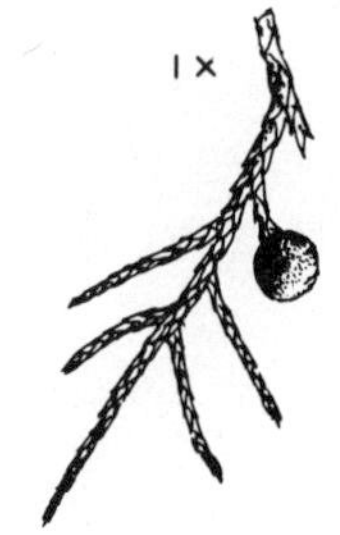

24. Southern red-cedar.

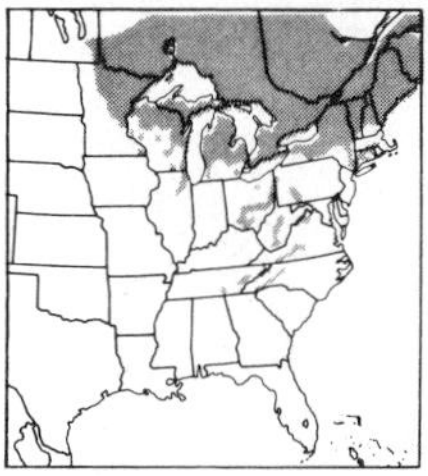

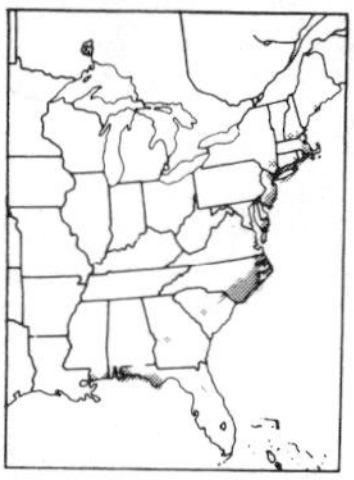

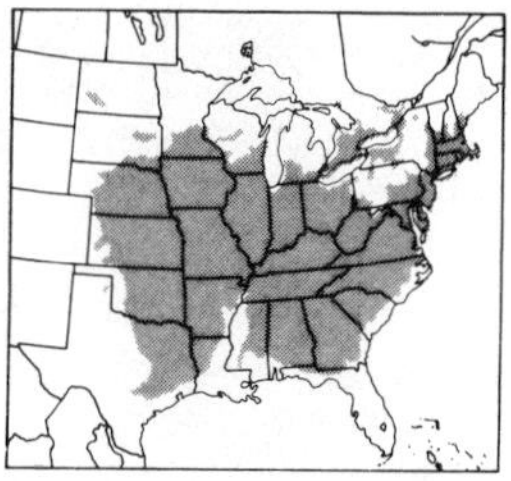

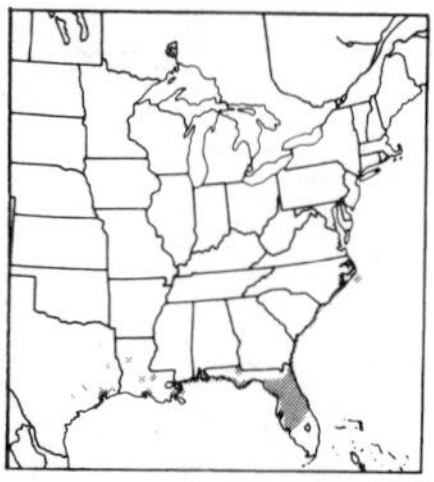

20. Fraser fir, *Abies fraseri* (Pursh) Poir. (balsam fir, eastern fir, Fraser balsam fir, southern balsam fir, balsam, she-balsam). Medium-sized tree of Appalachian Mountains in Virginia, North Carolina, and Tennessee. Bark gray or brown, thin, smoothish, with many resin blisters; bark on larger trunks with thin papery scales. Needles flat, $\frac{1}{2}$–1 in (12–25 mm) long, dark green, usually rounded at tip. Cones upright, $1\frac{1}{2}$–$2\frac{1}{2}$ in (4–6 cm) long, purple, with yellow-green bracts partly covering cone scales.

Principal uses: Same as No. 19.

DD. Leaves scalelike, less than $\frac{1}{4}$ in (6 mm) long (or needlelike and up to $\frac{3}{8}$ in (1 cm) long on leading shoots).

L. Leafy twigs more or less flattened; seeds in a hard cone.

M. Twigs much flattened, about $\frac{1}{8}$ in (3 mm) broad including leaves—**Thuja** (*Thuja*).

21. Northern white-cedar, *Thuja occidentalis* L. (white-cedar, eastern white-cedar, arborvitae, eastern arborvitae, swamp-cedar). Medium-sized tree of Northeastern United States, adjacent Canada, and Appalachian Mountain region. Bark reddish brown, thin, fibrous, with narrow connecting ridges. Twigs flattened and branching in one plane. Leaves appearing flattened in 2 rows, scalelike, $\frac{1}{16}$–$\frac{1}{8}$ in (1.5–3 mm) long, light yellow green, aromatic. Cones $\frac{3}{8}$–$\frac{1}{2}$ in (10–12 mm) long, pale brown.

Principal uses: Poles, railroad crossties, posts, and ornamental fencing. Lumber for boats, paneling, boxes, millwork, tanks, and building construction. Cedar-oil, used in medicine. Ornamental.

MM. Twigs slightly flattened, less than $\frac{1}{16}$ in (1.5 mm) broad including leaves—**White-cedar** (*Chamaecyparis*).

22. Atlantic white-cedar, *Chamaecyparis thyoides* (L.) B.S.P. (southern white-cedar, white-cedar, swamp-cedar). Medium-sized tree of swamps, Atlantic and Gulf Coastal Plains. Bark reddish brown, thin, fibrous, with narrow connecting ridges. Leafy twigs slightly flattened (or partly 4-angled). Leaves scalelike, $\frac{1}{16}$–$\frac{1}{8}$ in (1.5–3 mm) long, dull blue green. Cones $\frac{1}{4}$ in (6 mm) in diameter, bluish purple, with a bloom.

Principal uses: Boxes and crates, furniture, and industrial millwork. Ornamental.

LL. Leafy twigs rounded or 4-angled; seeds in a soft "berry"—**Juniper** (*Juniperus*).

23. Eastern redcedar, *Juniperus virginiana* L. (redcedar, red juniper). Medium-sized tree of eastern half of United States and adjacent Canada. Bark reddish brown, thin, fibrous and shreddy. Leafy twigs rounded or 4-angled, slender. Leaves scalelike, $\frac{1}{16}$ in (1.5 mm) long, dark blue green, or on leading shoots needlelike, up to $\frac{3}{8}$ in (10 mm) long. "Berry" $\frac{1}{4}-\frac{3}{8}$ in (6–10 mm) in diameter, dark blue.

Principal uses: Fence posts. Lumber for chests, wardrobes, and closet lining. Carvings. Cedar-leaf oil for medicine and cedar-wood oil for medicine and perfumes. Christmas trees. Shelterbelts and ornamental.

24. Southern redcedar, *Juniperus silicicola* (Small) Bailey (redcedar, sand-cedar, coast juniper). Medium-sized tree of South Atlantic and Gulf Coastal Plains. Bark reddish brown, thin, fibrous and shreddy. Leafy twigs rounded or 4-angled, very slender, usually hanging down. Leaves scalelike, $\frac{1}{16}$ in (1.5 mm) or less in length, dark blue green, or leaves on leading shoots needlelike. "Berry" $\frac{3}{16}$ in (5 mm) or less in diameter, dark blue.

Principal uses: Wood used same as No. 23. Ornamental.

ANGIOSPERMS (FLOWERING PLANTS)

AA (A on p. 5). Trees nonresinous, with leaves broad, shedding in fall in most species (evergreen in palmetto, holly, magnolia, live oak, etc.); seeds enclosed in fruit— **Angiosperms** (flowering plants).

MONOCOTYLEDONS

N. Leaves parallel-veined, evergreen clustered at top of trunk or large branches; trunk with woody portions irregularly distributed, without clear distinction of bark and wood, and without annual rings—**Monocotyledons** (palms, yuccas, etc.)

25. Cabbage palmetto, *Sabal palmetto* (Walt.) Lodd. ex. Schult. (palmetto, Carolina palmetto, cabbage-palm). Medium-sized palm tree of south Atlantic and Gulf coasts from North Carolina to Florida. Trunk stout and unbranched, grayish brown, roughened or ridged, with a cluster of large leaves at top. Leaves evergreen, coarse, fan-shaped, 4–7 ft (1.2–2.1 m) long, thick and leathery, much folded and divided into narrow segments with threadlike fibers hanging between. Leafstalks 5–8 ft (1.5–2.4 m) long. Fruits in much branched cluster about 7 ft (2.1 m) long, numerous, $\frac{3}{8}-\frac{1}{2}$ in (10–12 mm) in diameter, black, 1-seeded.

Principal uses: Trunks for wharf pilings, docks, and poles. Brushes and whiskbrooms are made from young leafstalk fibers; baskets, mats, hats, brooms and thatch are made from leaves. Ornamental. (State tree of Florida and South Carolina.)

DICOTYLEDONS (BROADLEAF TREES OR HARDWOODS)

NN. Leaves net-veined; trunk with bark and wood distinct and with annual rings in wood—**Dicotyledons** (broadleaf trees or hardwoods, such as oaks, poplars, ashes, maples).

O. (OO on p. 15). Leaves and usually branches in pairs (opposite; or in 3's in No 27; see also No. 64).

P. Leaves not divided into leaflets (simple).

Q. Leaf edges straight or curved, not toothed or lobed.

R. Leaves slightly thick and leathery, with inconspicuous side veins, evergreen (tropical tree of Florida)—**Mangrove** (*Rhizophora mangle*).

26. Mangrove, *Rhizophora mangle* L. (red mangrove; mangle, mangle colorado, Puerto Rico). Small to large evergreen tree on silt shores of southern Florida including Florida Keys; coasts of tropical America from Bermuda, West Indies, and Mexico south to Brazil and Peru; introduced in Hawaii. Stilt roots curved, arched, and branching above water. Bark gray or gray brown, smooth becoming furrowed. Leaves paired or opposite, elliptic, $2\frac{1}{2}-4$ in (6–10 cm) long, blunt-pointed at apex and short-pointed at base, hairless, shiny green above, yellow green beneath, slightly leathery and fleshy. Fruits distinctive, dark brown, about $1\frac{1}{4}$ in (3 cm) long, containing a growing cigar-like brown seedling to 1 ft (30 cm) long, hanging down and falling.

Principal uses: Lumber, shipbuilding, cabinetwork. Marine piling. Bark for tannin.

RR. Leaves thin, with prominent side veins, shedding in fall.

S. Leaves heart-shaped, large, more than 6 in (15 cm) long, in 3's or pairs— **Catalpa** (*Catalpa*).

27. Northern catalpa, *Catalpa speciosa* Warder ex Engelm. (western catalpa, hardy catalpa, cigartree, western catawba-tree). Medium-sized to large tree of lower Ohio Valley and central Mississippi Valley, naturalized elsewhere in Eastern United States. Bark reddish brown, with flat, scaly ridges. Leaves in 3's or paired, large, heart-shaped, 6–12 in (15–30 cm) long, long-pointed, edges not toothed, thick, dark green above hairy beneath. Leafstalk 4–6 in (10–15 cm) long. Flowers large and showy, about 2 in (5 cm) long, whitish and purple spotted. Fruiting capsule cigarlike, long and narrow, 8–18 in (20–45 cm) long and

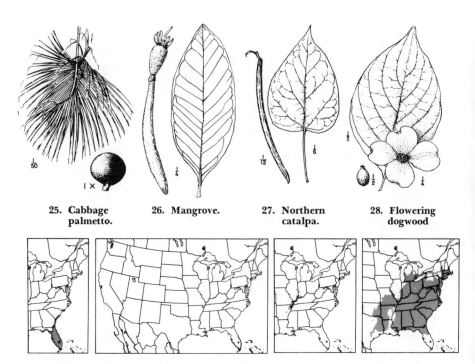

25. Cabbage palmetto. **26. Mangrove.** **27. Northern catalpa.** **28. Flowering dogwood**

⅝ in (1.5 cm) thick, dark brown, with many winged seeds.

Principal uses: Fence posts. Shade tree and ornamental. Shelterbelts.

SS. Leaves elliptic, less than 6 in (15 cm) long—**Dogwood** (*Cornus*).

28. Flowering dogwood, *Cornus florida* L. (dogwood cornel, boxwood; *Cynoxylon floridum* (L.) Raf.). Small tree of eastern half of United States; also in southern Ontario and a variety in Eastern Mexico. Bark dark reddish brown, broken into small square or rounded blocks. Leaves paired, elliptic, 3–6 in (7.5–15 cm) long, short-pointed, edges appearing straight but minutely toothed, side veins curved, bright green and nearly hairless above, whitish and slightly hairy beneath, turning scarlet in fall. Flowers greenish yellow, in a dense head with 4 showy, white, petallike bracts 2¼–4 in (6–10 cm) in diameter, in early spring. Fruits egg-shaped, ⅜ in (1 cm) long, scarlet, shiny, fleshy, 1- or 2-seeded.

Principal uses: Important ornamental. The outstanding wood for shuttles (used in textile weaving). Also spools, small pulleys, mallet heads, and jeweler's blocks. (State tree of Missouri. State flower of North Carolina and Virginia.)

QQ. Leaf edges toothed, deeply 3- or 5-lobed (fruit of paired, long-winged "keys") —**Maple** (*Acer*).

T. Teeth of leaves few and blunt—**Hard maples.**

29. Sugar maple, *Acer saccharum* Marsh. (rock maple, hard maple; *A. saccharophorum* K. Koch). Large tree of eastern half of United States and adjacent Canada. Bark gray, furrowed into irregular ridges or scales. Leaves paired, heart-shaped, 3–5½ in (7.5–14 cm) in diameter, the 3 or 5 lobes long-pointed and coarsely toothed with few blunt teeth, dark green above, light green or pale and usually hairless beneath, turning yellow, orange, or scarlet in fall. Key fruits 1–1¼ in (2.5–3 cm) long, maturing in fall.

Principal uses: As a group, maples rank third in production of hardwood lumber, next to oak and sweetgum, and among the leading furniture woods. Sugar maple is used for flooring, furniture, boxes and crates, shoe lasts, handles, woodenware and novelties, spools and bobbins; and truck, trailer, and railroad car parts; and bowling pins and alleys. Also veneer, railroad crossties, charcoal, and pulpwood. Sugar maple is the commercial source of maple sugar and sirup. Much planted as a shade tree. (State tree of New York, Vermont, West Virginia, and Wisconsin.)

30. Black maple, *Acer nigrum* Michx. f. (black sugar maple, sugar maple, hard maple; *A. saccharum* var. *nigrum* (Michx. f.) Britton). Large tree of northeastern quarter of United States and adjacent Canada. Bark gray, becoming deeply furrowed. Leaves paired, heart-

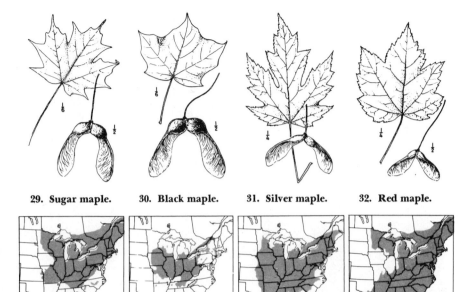

29. Sugar maple.   **30. Black maple.**   **31. Silver maple.**   **32. Red maple.**

shaped, 4–5½ in (10–14 cm) in diameter, 3-lobed or occasionally 5-lobed, lobes short-pointed and coarsely toothed with few blunt teeth, the sides dropping, dull green above, yellowish green and hairy beneath, turning yellow in fall, leafstalks hairy. Key fruits 1–1¼ in (2.5–3 cm) long, maturing in fall. (Perhaps only a variety of No. 29.)

Principal uses: Same as No. 29.

TT. Teeth of leaves many and sharp—**Soft maples.**

31. Silver maple, *Acer saccharinum* L. (soft maple, white maple, river maple, water maple, swamp maple.) Large tree of eastern half of United States and adjacent Canada. Bark gray, thin, smooth, on large trunks broken into long, thin scales. Leaves paired, slightly heart-shaped, 3–6 in (7.5–15 cm) long, deeply 5-lobed, lobes long-pointed, deeply, sharply, and irregularly toothed bright green above, silvery white beneath, turning yellow in fall. Key friuts 1½–2½ in (4–6 cm) long, maturing in spring.

Principal uses: Furniture, boxes and crates, handles, woodenware and novelties, and spools and bobbins. Also distillation products and pulpwood. Shade tree. Shelterbelts.

32. Red maple, *Acer rubrum* L. (scarlet maple, soft maple, swamp maple, Carolina red maple, water maple, white maple). Large tree of eastern half of United States and adjacent Canada. Bark gray, thin, smooth, on large trunks broken into long, thin scales. Twigs reddish. Leaves paired, heart-shaped, 2½–4 in (6–10 cm) long, the 3 or 5 lobes short-pointed, irregularly and sharply toothed, dark green and shiny above, whitish and slightly hairy beneath, turning scarlet or yellow in fall. Key fruits ¾ in (2 cm) long, maturing in spring.

Principal uses: Same as No. 31. (State tree of Rhode Island.)

PP. Leaves divided into 3–11 leaflets (compound).
    U. Leaflets attached along extended leafstalk (pinnate).
       V. Leaflets 3–7, sharply toothed, with veins extending to teeth (fruits paired, clustered, long-winged "keys")—**Boxelder** (*Acer negundo*).

33. Boxelder, *Acer negundo* L. (California boxelder, ashleaf maple, Manitoba maple, boxelder maple). Medium sized tree, including its varieties widely distributed across the United States and adjacent Canada. Bark gray or brown, thin, with narrow ridges and fissures. Twigs green. Leaves paired, compound, with usually 3 or 5, rarely 7 or 9, oval or lance-oblong leaflets 2–4 in (5–10 cm) long, long-pointed, coarsely and sharply toothed, bright green, nearly smooth or hairy. Key fruits 1–1½ in (2.5–4 cm) long, paired and in clusters, maturing in fall.

Principal uses: Shelterbelts. Shade tree.

13

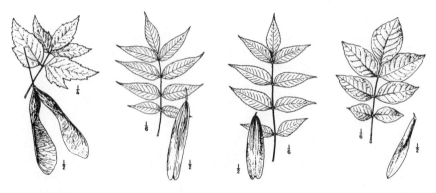

33. Boxelder.   **34. Black ash.**   **35. Blue ash.**   **36. White ash.**

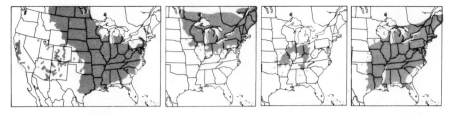

VV. Leaflets 5–11, bluntly toothed or without teeth, with veins curved within edges (fruits clustered but not in pairs, long-winged "keys")—**Ash** (*Fraxinus*).
     W. Leaflets without stalks.

34. Black ash, *Fraxinus nigra* Marsh. (swamp ash, water ash, brown ash, hoop ash, basket ash). Medium-sized to large tree of wet soils in northeastern quarter of United States and adjacent Canada. Bark gray, scaly or fissured. Leaves paired, compound, 12–16 in (30–40 cm) long, with 7–11 stalkless, oblong or broadly lance-shaped leaflets 3–5 in (7.5–13 cm) long, long-pointed, finely toothed, with tufted hairs beneath. Key fruits 1–1½ in (2.5–4 cm) long, ⅜ in (1 cm) wide, flat, with wing extending to base.
Principal uses: Same as No. 36.

    WW. Leaflets with stalks.

35. Blue ash, *Fraxinus quadrangulata* Michx. Medium-sized to large tree of Central States, chiefly Ohio and Mississippi Valley regions; also in southern Ontario. Bark gray, fissured, with scaly and shaggy plates. Twigs 4-angled and more or less winged. Leaves paired, compound, 8–12 in (20–30 cm) long, with 7–11 short-stalked, oval or lance-shaped leaflets 2½–5 in (6–13 cm) long, long-pointed, toothed. Key fruits 1¼–2 in (3–5 cm) long, ⅜–½ in (1–1.2 cm) wide, oblong, with wing extending to base.
Principal uses: Same as No. 36.

36. White ash, *Fraxinus americana* L. (American ash, Biltmore ash; *F. biltmoreana* Beadle). Large tree of eastern half of United States and adjacent Canada. Bark gray, with deep, diamond-shaped fissures and narrow, forking ridges. Leaves paired, compound, 8–12 in (20–30 cm) long, with 5–9, usually 7, stalked, oval or broadly lance-shaped leaflets 2½–5 in (6–13 cm) long, long- or short-pointed, edges sometimes slightly toothed, hairless or hairy beneath. Key fruits 1–2 in (2.5–5 cm) long and ¼ in (6 mm) wide, with wing at end.
Principal uses: Furniture, flooring, millwork, paneling, sporting and athletic goods, handtools, and boxes and crates. Shade tree.

37. Green ash, *Fraxinus pennsylvanica* Marsh. (red ash, Darlington ash, white ash, swamp ash, water ash; *F. viridis* Michx. f.). Medium-sized to large tree of eastern half of United States and adjacent Canada west to Montana and Texas. Bark gray, fissured. Leaves paired, compound, 10–12 in (25–30 cm) long, with 7 or 9 stalked, oval or lance-shaped leaflets 2–6 in (5–15 cm) long, long-pointed, slightly toothed, hairless or hairy beneath. Key fruits 1¼–2¼ in (3–6 cm) long, ¼ in (6 mm) or more in width, with wing extending nearly to base.
Principal uses: Same as No. 36. Also shelterbelts and shade tree.

14

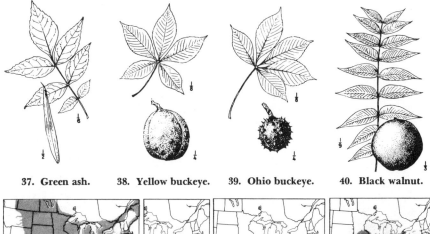

37. Green ash.   38. Yellow buckeye.   39. Ohio buckeye.   40. Black walnut.

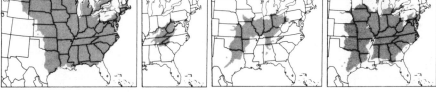

UU. Leaflets 5 (to 7), all attached end of leafstalk and spreading fingerlike (palmate)—**Buckeye** (*Aesculus*).

38. Yellow buckeye, *Aesculus octandra* Marsh. (sweet buckeye, big buckeye). Medium-sized to large tree of Central States, chiefly Ohio Valley and Appalachian regions. Bark gray, separating into thin scales. Leaves paired, compound, with leafstalks 4–6 in (10–15 cm) long. Leaflets 5, oblong or elliptic, 4–6 in (10–15 cm) long, long-pointed, narrowed at base, finely toothed. Flowers in branched clusters 4–6 in (10–15 cm) long, showy, 1¼ in (3 cm) long, yellow with petals unequal. Fruiting capsule 2–2½ in (5–6 cm) in diameter, smooth, with 2 poisonous seeds 1½–1¾ in (4–4.5 cm) wide.

Principal uses: Lumber for furniture, boxes, crating, trunks, signs, and flooring; scientific instrument cases, novelties, woodenware, and musical instruments. Also limited use in food containers, drawing boards, plaques, and carvings. Ornamental.

39. Ohio buckeye, *Aesculus glabra* Willd. (fetid buckeye, stinking buckeye, American horsechestnut). Small tree (or shrubby to medium-sized) of Central States, chiefly Ohio and Mississippi Valley regions. Bark gray, much furrowed and broken into scaly plates. Leaves paired, compound, with leafstalks 4–6 in (10–15 cm) long. Leaflets 5 (5–7 in shrubby varieties), elliptic, 3–5 in (7.5–13 cm) long, long-pointed, narrowed at base, finely toothed. Flowers in branched clusters 4–6 in (10–15 cm) long, showy, ¾–1¼ in (2–3 cm) long, pale greenish yellow, with petals nearly equal in length. Fruiting capsule 1¼–2 in (3–5 cm) in diameter, prickly, with 1 or 2 poisonous seeds 1–1½ in (2.5–4 cm) wide.

Principal uses: Same as No. 38.   (State tree of Ohio.)

OO (O on p. 11). Leaves and usually branches borne singly (alternate).
   X (XX on p. 20). Leaves divided into leaflets (compound), attached along extended leafstalk (pinnate).
      Y. Leaflets long-pointed; twigs not spiny; fruit rounded, egg-shaped, or oblong.
      Z. Leaflets finely toothed, shedding in fall; fruit a nut with a husk.
         a. Leaflets mostly 11–21; pith of twigs in plates; husk of nut not splitting off—
            Walnut (*Juglans*).

40. Black walnut, *Juglans nigra* L. (eastern black walnut, American walnut). Large tree of eastern half of United States and southern Ontario. Bark dark brown to black, thick, with deep furrows and narrow, forking ridges. Compound leaves 12–24 in (30–60 cm) long. Leaflets 9–21, without stalks, broadly lance-shaped, 2½–5 in (6–13 cm) long, long-pointed, finely toothed, nearly hairless above, soft hairy beneath. Nuts single or paired, 1½–2½ in (4–6 cm) in diameter including thick husk, nearly round, irregularly ridged, thick-shelled,

15

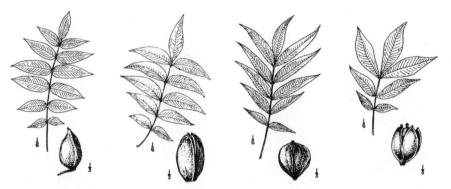

41. Butternut.   **42. Pecan.**   **43. Water hickory.**   **44. Nutmeg hickory.**

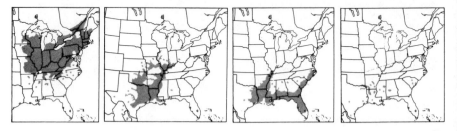

sweet and edible, known as walnuts.

Principal uses: Valuable furniture wood, solid and as veneer. Radio, television, and phonograph cabinets; sewing machines, gunstocks, and interior finish. Edible walnuts. Shade tree. Shelterbelts.

41. Butternut, *Juglans cinerea* L. (white walnut, oilnut). Medium-sized to large tree of northeastern quarter of United States and adjacent Canada. Bark light gray, furrowed into broad, flat ridges. Compound leaves 15–24 in (38–60 cm) long. Leaflets 7–17, without stalks, broadly lanced-shaped, 2–4½ in (5–11 cm) long, long- or short-pointed, finely toothed, slightly hairy above, soft hairy beneath. Nuts 3–5 in drooping clusters, 1½–2½ in (4–6 cm) long including thick husk, egg-shaped, pointed, irregularly ridged, thick-shelled, sweet and oily, known as butternuts.

Principal uses: Furniture. Shade tree. Edible butternuts.

> aa. Leaflets 5–11 (11–17 in No. 42); pith of twigs solid; husk of nut splitting off—**Hickory** (*Carya;* formerly known also as *Hicoria*).
> b. Leaflets lance-shaped and often slightly sickle-shaped; winter buds with 4–6 scales, fitting at edges and not overlapping; nuts thin-shelled (except No. 44), husks usually 4-winged—**Pecan hickories.**

42. Pecan, *Carya illinoensis* (Wangenh.) K. Koch (sweet pecan; *C. pecan* (Marsh.) Engl. & Graebn., not (Walt.) Nutt.). Large tree of Mississippi Valley region; also in Mexico. Bark light brown or gray, deeply and irregularly furrowed and cracked. Compound leaves 12–20 in (30–50 cm) long. Leaflets 11–17, short-stalked, lance-shaped and slightly sickle-shaped, 2–7 in (5–18 cm) long, long-pointed, finely toothed, hairless or slightly hairy. Nuts 1–2 in (2.5–5 cm) long including slightly 4-winged, thin husk, oblong, pointed, thin-shelled, sweet and edible, known as pecans.

Principal uses: Furniture and flooring. Specialty items such as novelties and sporting goods. Veneer for paneling and plywood containers. Fuelwood and charcoal for smoking meats. Pecan nuts from wild and cultivated trees. Shade tree. (State tree of Texas.)

43. Water hickory, *Carya aquatica* (Michx. f.) Nutt. (bitter pecan, swamp hickory, bitter water hickory, wild pecan, pecan). Medium-sized or large tree of wet soils in South Atlantic coast. Gulf coast, and Mississippi Valley regions. Bark light brown, fissured, with long, thin scales. Compound leaves 9–15 in (23–38 cm) long. Leaflets 7–13, stalkless or short-stalked, lance-shaped, 2–5 in (5–13 cm) long, long-pointed, finely toothed, dark green above, brownish and often hairy beneath. Nuts 1–1½ in long including pointed, 4-winged, thin husk, rounded but flattened, angled, and wrinkled, thin-shelled, bitter.

Principal uses: Wood used same as No. 42.

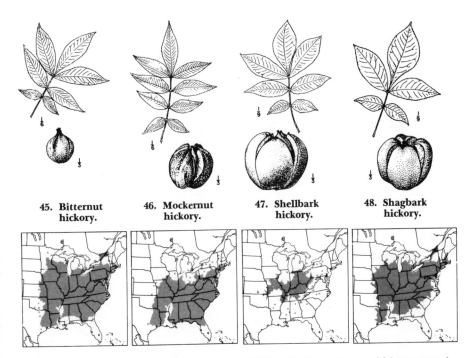

45. Bitternut hickory.   **46. Mockernut hickory.**   **47. Shellbark hickory.**   **48. Shagbark hickory.**

44. Nutmeg hickory, *Carya myristiciformis* (Michx. f.) Nutt. (swamp hickory, pecan). Large tree of South Atlantic coast and Gulf coast regions; also in Mexico. Bark dark brown, fissured, with small, thin scales. Compound leaves 7–14 in (18–36 cm) long. Leaflets 5–9, short-stalked, broadly lance-shaped or oblong, 2–5 in (5–13 cm) long, long-pointed, finely toothed, dark green above, more or less hairy and whitish beneath. Nuts 1¼–1½ in (3–4 cm) long including pointed, 4-winged, thin husk, nearly round but longer than broad, thick-shelled, sweet and edible.
Principal uses: Wood used same as No. 42. Edible hickory nuts.

45. Bitternut hickory, *Carya cordiformis* (Wangenh.) K. Koch (bitternut, pignut, swamp hickory, pecan). Medium-sized to large tree of eastern half of United States and adjacent Canada. Bark light brown, shallowly furrowed, with narrow, forking ridges or thin scales. Compound leaves 6–10 in (15–20 cm) long. Leaflets 5–9, without stalks, lance-shaped, 2–6 in (5–15 cm) long, long-pointed, finely toothed, more or less hairy beneath. Winter buds bright yellow. Nuts ¾–1¼ in (2–3 cm) long including 4-winged, yellowish, thin husk, nearly round, slightly flattened, short-pointed, thin-shelled, bitter.
Principal uses: Wood used same as No. 42.

bb. Leaflets oblong to broadly lance-shaped; winter buds with more than 6 overlapping scales; nuts thick-shelled (except Nos. 48 and 49), husks without wings—**True hickories.**

46. Mockernut hickory, *Carya tomentosa* Nutt. (mockernut, white hickory, whiteheart hickory, bullnut, hognut). Medium-sized to large tree of eastern half of United States except northern border; also in southern Ontario. Bark gray, irregularly furrowed into flat ridges. Compound leaves 8–20 in (10–50 cm) long. Leaflets 7 or 9, without stalks, oblong or broadly lance-shaped, 2–8 in (5–20 cm) long, long-pointed, finely toothed, dark yellow green and shiny above, pale and densely hairy beneath. Nuts 1½–2 in (4–5 cm) long including thick husk, nearly round, slightly flattened and angled, thick-shelled, sweet and edible.
Principal uses: Furniture, flooring, tool handles, ladders, specialty items, and sporting goods such as baseball bats, skis, and archery equipment. Veneer for paneling and plywood. Fuelwood, charcoal, for smoking meats. Hickory nuts.

47. Shellbark hickory, *Carya laciniosa* (Michx. f.) Loud. (big shagbark hickory, kingnut, big shellbark, western shellbark, thick shellbark, bottom shellbark). Large tree of Ohio and Mississippi Valley regions. Bark gray, shaggy with long, thin, straight plates. Compound leaves 15–22 in (38–56 cm) long. Leaflets usually 7, without stalks or short-stalked, broadly lance-shaped, 2–8 in (5–20 cm) long, long-pointed, finely toothed, dark green and shiny

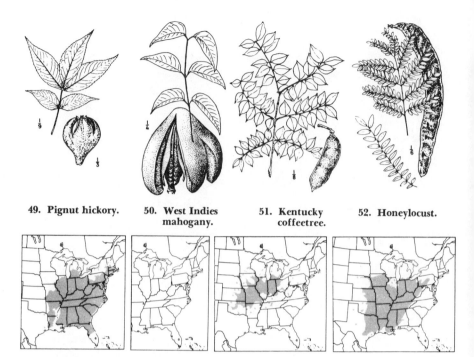

49. Pignut hickory. **50. West Indies mahogany.** **51. Kentucky coffeetree.** **52. Honeylocust.**

above, pale and soft-hairy beneath. Nuts 1¾–2½ in (4.5–6 cm) long including thick husk, nearly round, slightly flattened and angled, pointed at ends, thick-shelled, sweet and edible.
Principal uses: Same as No. 46.

48. Shagbark hickory, *Carya ovata* (Mill.) K. Koch (shellbark hickory, southern shagbark hickory, upland hickory, Carolina hickory, shagbark). Large tree of eastern half of United States and adjacent Canada. Bark gray, shaggy with long, thin, curved plates. Compound leaves 8–14 in (20–36 cm) long. Leaflets usually 5, stalkless elliptic or broadly lance-shaped, 3–7 in (7.5–18 cm) long, long-pointed, finely toothed. Nuts 1¼–2½ in (3–6 cm) long including thick husk, nearly round, slightly flattened and angled, thin-shelled, sweet and edible.
Principal uses: Same as No. 46. Wild trees and improved cultivated varieties produce hickory nuts of commerce.

49. Pignut hickory, *Carya glabra* (Mill.) Sweet (pignut, oval pignut hickory, sweet pignut). Variety: red hickory, var. *odorata* (Marsh.) Little (*C. ovalis* (Wangenh.) Sarg.). Large tree of eastern third of United States and southern Ontario. Bark dark gray, with furrows and forking ridges. Compound leaves 8–12 in (20–30 cm) long. Leaflets usually 5, or 5 and 7, stalkless, oblong or lance-shaped, 3–6 in (7.5–15 cm) long, long-pointed, finely toothed, hairless. Nuts 1–2 in (2.5–5 cm) long including thin or thick husk, broader toward apex and usually not angled, thin- or thick-shelled, usually bitter.
Principal uses: Same as No. 46.

    ZZ. Leaflets without teeth on edges, evergreen; fruit egg-shaped with winged seeds (tree of tropical Florida)—**Mahogany** (*Swietenia*).

50. West Indies mahogany, *Swietenia mahagoni* Jacq. (mahogany). Medium-sized to large tree, rare in extreme southern Florida including Florida Keys; also in West Indies. Bark dark reddish brown, fissured. Leaves compound, evergreen, 4–6 in (10–15 cm) long. Leaflets 4–8, paired, short-stalked, broadly lance-shaped, 1½–3 in (4–7.5 cm) long. Leaflets 4–8, paired short-stalked, broadly lance-shaped, 1½–3 in (4–7.5 cm) long, long-pointed, the 2 sides unequal, leathery, without teeth on edges, yellow green, hairless. Flowers small, in clusters, whitish green. Fruit a large egg-shaped capsule 3–5 in (7.5–13 cm) long, dark brown, with winged seeds 1¾ in (4.5 cm) long.
Principal uses: Not of commercial importance in Florida because of its rarity. Mahogany, including other species, is the world's foremost cabinetwood and one of the most valuable timber trees in tropical America. Planted as an ornamental and shade tree in Florida, Puerto Rico, Virgin Islands, and Hawaii.

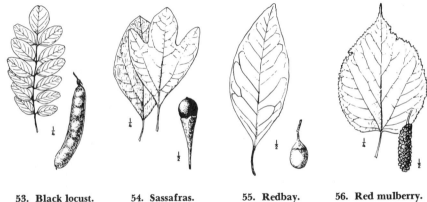

53. Black locust. 54. Sassafras. 55. Redbay. 56. Red mulberry.

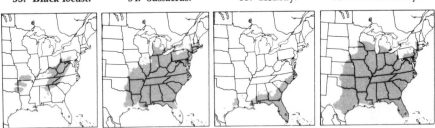

YY. Leaflets blunt-pointed or rounded; twigs spiny (except in No. 51); fruit a flat beanlike pod.
    c. Leaflets blunt-pointed, more than 2 in (5 cm) long—**Kentucky coffeetree** (*Gymnocladus dioicus*).

51. Kentucky coffeetree, *Gymnocladus dioicus* (L.) K. Koch (coffeetree). Large tree of northeastern and central United States. Bark gray, deeply furrowed into narrow ridges. Leaves very large, twice divided (compound), 1–3 ft (30–90 cm) long, with 5–9 pairs of side axes. Leaflets many in pairs, short-stalked, oval, 1½–2½ in (4–6 cm) long, short-pointed, nearly hairless, turning yellow in fall. Flowers greenish white, ¾ in (20 mm) long, many in branching clusters, mostly male and female on different trees. Pods 5–6 in (13–15 cm) long and 1½–2 in (4–5 cm) wide, dark brown, thick, with large rounded seeds.
    Principal uses: Cabinetwork. Ornamental. Seeds formerly used as coffee substitute.

    cc. Leaflets rounded at apex, less than 2 in (5 cm) long.
        d. Leaflets with inconspicuous rounded teeth—**Honeylocust** (*Gleditsia*).

52. Honeylocust, *Gleditsia triacanthos* L. (sweet-locust, thorny-locust). Large tree of Appalachian Mountain and Mississippi Valley regions, naturalized elsewhere in eastern half of United States; also in extreme southern Ontario. Bark grayish brown or black, fissured into long, narrow, scaly ridges. Trunk and branches with large, stout, usually branched spines, rarely absent. Leaves once or twice divided (compound), 4–8 in (10–20 cm) long. Leaflets numerous in pairs, elliptic, ⅜–1¼ in (1–3 cm) long, blunt-pointed or rounded at apex, with inconspicuous rounded teeth, shiny dark green and hairless above, yellow green and nearly hairless beneath. Flowers small, greenish or whitish, in narrow clusters 2–2½ in (5–6 cm) long, in late spring. Pods 12–18 in (30–45 cm) long and 1–1¼ in (2.5–3 cm) wide, flat, dark brown, hairy, slightly curved and twisted.
    Principal uses: Wood used locally for fence posts, construction, furniture, and railroad crossties. Shade tree. Shelterbelts. The sweetish pods are eaten by livestock and wildlife.

    dd. Leaflets not toothed—**Locust** (*Robinia*).

53. Black locust, *Robinia pseudoacacia* L. (locust, yellow locust, shipmast locust). Medium-sized tree, native in Appalachian Mountain and Ozark regions and widely naturalized in eastern half of United States and southern Canada. Bark brown, deeply furrowed, with rough, forked ridges. Twigs with paired spines about ½ in (12 mm) long developing at base of each leaf. Compound leaves 8–14 in (20–36 cm) long. Leaflets 7–19, elliptic, 1–2 in (2.5–5 cm) long, usually rounded at apex, not toothed, dark blue green and hairless above, pale and hairless or nearly so beneath. Flowers white and very fragrant,

19

beanlike, ⅝–¾ in (15–20 mm) long, in clusters 4–8 in (10–20 cm) long, in spring. Pods 2–4 in (5–10 cm) long and ½ in (1.2 cm) wide, flat, brown.

Principal uses: Fenceposts, mine timbers; flooring and furniture. The principal wood for insulator pins. Planted for ornament and shade, shelterbelts, and erosion control, such as on land strip-mined for coal.

    XX (X on p. 15). Leaves not divided into leaflets (simple).
      e. Leaves aromatic when bruised; twigs greenish (see also No. 58).
        f. Leaves partly 2- or 3-lobed, thin, shedding in fall—**Sassafras** (*Sassafras albidum*).

54. Sassafras, *Sassafras albidum* (Nutt.) Nees (*S. officinale* Nees & Eberm., *S. variifolium* (Salisb.) Kuntze). Medium-sized tree (sometimes large) with aromatic odor and taste, eastern half of United States and southern Ontario. Bark reddish brown, deeply furrowed. Leaves oval or elliptic, 3–5 in (7.5–13 cm) long, blunt-pointed, often 2- or 3-lobed but not toothed, bright green above, paler and often hairy beneath, turning orange or scarlet in fall. Flowers about ⅜ in (1 cm) long, yellow, in small clusters in early spring. Fruits egg-shaped, ⅜ in (1 cm) long, dark blue, with fleshy red stalk.

Principal uses: Boats, oars, general millwork, exterior and interior trim. Fence posts. Lumber occasionally mixed with that of black ash (No. 34). Sassafras tea and oil of sassafras, used to perfume soap, are prepared from roots and root bark. Shade tree and ornamental.

       ff. Leaves not lobed, slightly thickened, evergreen—**Persea** (*Persea*).

55. Redbay, *Persea borbonia* (L.) Spreng. (variety: swampbay, *P. palustris* (Raf.) Sarg.). Medium-sized tree of Coastal Plain of Southeastern United States. Bark dark reddish brown, irregularly furrowed into small thick scales. Leaves evergreen, oblong or elliptic, 3–5 in (7.5–13 cm) long, blunt-pointed at apex, short-pointed at base, edges rolled under, thick and leathery, shiny green above, beneath whitish or with rusty hairs. Flowers several in long-stalked cluster, pale yellow, ⅛–¼ in (3–6 mm) long. Fruits rounded, ½ in (12 mm) in diameter, shiny dark blue black, 1-seeded.

Principal uses: cabinet-making, lumber.

      ee. Leaves not aromatic; twigs mostly brown or gray.
        g. Juice milky.
          h. Leaves toothed, sometimes 2- or 3-lobed; twigs not spiny—**Mulberry** (*Morus*).

56. Red mulberry, *Morus rubra* L. Medium-sized tree of eastern half of United States and southern Ontario. Bark dark brown, fissured and scaly. Leaves broadly oval or heart-shaped, 3–7 in (7.5–18 cm) long, abruptly long-pointed, coarsely toothed, sometimes 2- or 3-lobed, rough above, soft-hairy beneath. Fruits 1 in (2.5 cm) long, dark purple or black, sweet, juicy, and edible, known as mulberries.

Principal uses: Wood used locally for fence posts, furniture, interior finish, agricultural implements, and cooperage. Shade tree. Edible mulberries, eaten also by domestic animals and wildlife.

          hh. Leaves without teeth on edges; twigs spiny—**Osage-orange** (*Maclura*).

57. Osage-orange, *Maclura pomifera* (Raf.) Schneid. (bodark, bois-d'arc, mockorange, bow-wood, hedge, hedge-apple, horse-apple; *Toxylon promiferum* Raf.). Medium-sized tree with milky juice or sap, native of Arkansas, Oklahoma, Louisiana, and Texas but naturalized in eastern half of United States except northern border and introduced in West. Bark orange brown, deeply furrowed. Twigs with stout straight spines ⅜–1 in (1–2.5 cm) long. Leaves oval or narrowly oval, 2–5 in (5–13 cm) long, long-pointed, without teeth on edges, shiny dark green above and paler beneath, hairless. Fruit a yellow green ball 4–5 in (10–13 cm) in diameter.

Principal uses: Extensively planted for shelterbelts, hedges, ornament, and shade. Fence-posts and fuel, formerly archery bows and source of a yellow dye.

        gg. Juice or sap watery.
          i. (ii on p. 32). Winter buds 1 or none at tip of twig; pith of twigs round or nearly so in cross section (star-shaped in Nos. 81–84 and 98); fruit not an acorn.
           j. Leaves with 3–6 lobes.
             k. Leaves with pointed apex and 3 or 5 lobes.
               l. Leaves star-shaped, deeply 5-lobed—**Sweetgum** (*Liquidambar styraciflua*).

58. Sweetgum, *Liquidambar styraciflua* L. (redgum, sapgum, starleaf-gum, bilsted). Large tree of eastern third of United States, except northern border; also a variety in Mexico and Central America south to Nicaragua. Bark gray, deeply furrowed. Twigs reddish brown,

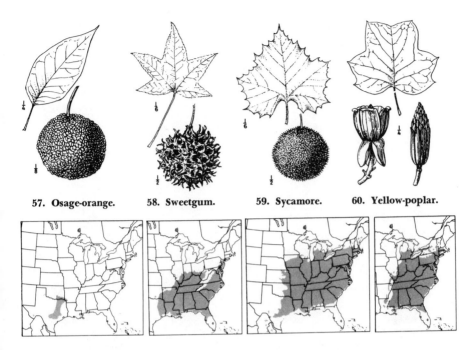

57. Osage-orange. **58. Sweetgum.** **59. Sycamore.** **60. Yellow-poplar.**

developing corky ridges. Leaves maplelike, star-shaped, 3–7 in (7.5–18 cm) long and wide, with 5 long-pointed, finely toothed lobes, shiny dark green above, paler beneath, nearly hairless, slightly aromatic, turning deep crimson in fall. Fruit a brownish, spiny ball 1–1¼ in (2.5–3 cm) in diameter.

Principal uses: Important timber tree in United States, second in production among hardwoods and one of leading woods for furniture and veneer. Lumber, veneer, plywood, pulpwood, and slack cooperage. Boxes and crates, containers, and prefabricated products. Shade tree. The gum, "sweetgum" or storax, is used in perfumes and medicines.

   ll. Leaves heart-shaped, slightly 3-lobed—**Sycamore** (*Platanus*).

 59. Sycamore, *Platanus occidentalis* L. (planetree, buttonwood, American sycamore, American planetree, buttonball-tree). Very large tree (largest eastern hardwood in trunk diameter) of wet soils in eastern half of United States and southern Ontario. Bark of branches whitish, thin, smooth; bark of trunk peeling off in large flakes, smoothish, with patches of brown, green, and gray. Leaves heart-shaped, 4–8 in (10–20 cm) long and wide, slightly 3- or 5-lobed, the shallow, pointed lobes coarsely toothed with long-pointed teeth, with 3 main veins from base, bright green and hairless above, paler and slightly hairy beneath. Many minute hairy fruits in ball 1 in (2.5 cm) in diameter.

Principal uses: Furniture parts, boxes (especially food containers), millwork, flooring, and hardwood dimension products. Specialty products, such as butcher blocks and handles for brushes and brooms. Pulpwood, particleboard, and wood fiberboard. Shade tree.

   kk. Leaves with broad, slightly notched apex and 4 or 6 lobes—**Yellow-poplar** (*Liriodendron tulipifera*).

 60. Yellow-poplar, *Liriodendron tulipifera* L. (tuliptree, tulip-poplar, "poplar," white-poplar, whitewood). Large tree (tallest eastern hardwood) of eastern third of United States and southern Ontario. Bark brown, becoming thick and deeply furrowed. Leaves of unusual squarish shape with broad, slightly notched or nearly straight apex and 2 or 3 lobes on each side, 3–6 in (7.5–15 cm) long, long and broad, shiny dark green above and pale green beneath, hairless. Flowers large and showy, tulip-shaped, 1½–2 in (4–5 cm) in diameter, greenish and orange, in spring. Fruit conelike, 2½–3 in (6–7.5 cm) long, ½ in (1.2 cm) thick.

Principal uses: One of the chief commercial hardwood species, third in volume of lumber used in furniture industry. Furniture (solid and veneer), fixtures, boxes and crates, millwork. Also musical instruments, caskets, toys, and sporting goods. Pulpwood. Ornamental and shade tree. (State tree of Indiana, Kentucky, and Tennessee.)

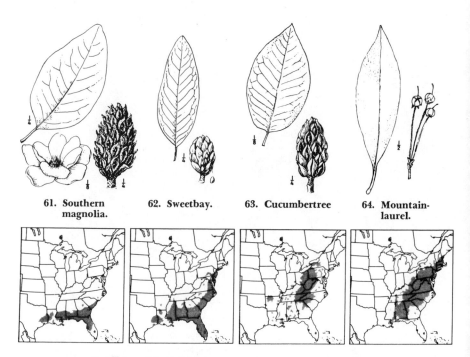

61. Southern magnolia.   **62. Sweetbay.**   **63. Cucumbertree**   **64. Mountain-laurel.**

jj. Leaves without lobes.
  m. Leaf edges without teeth.
    n. Twigs with faint ring at base of each leaf—**Magnolia** (*Magnolia*).

61. Southern magnolia, *Magnolia grandiflora* L. (evergreen magnolia). Medium-sized to large tree of South Atlantic and Gulf Coastal plains. Bark gray or light brown, broken into small, thin scales. Leaves evergreen, oblong or elliptic, 5–8 in (13–20 cm) long, short-pointed, edges without teeth, leathery, shiny bright green and hairless above, rusty-hairy beneath. Flowers cup-shaped, very large, 6–8 in (15–20 cm) across, white, fragrant, spring and summer. Fruit conelike, 3–4 in (7.5–10 cm) long, 1½–2½ in (4–6 cm) thick, rusty-hairy.

Principal uses: Furniture, boxes and other containers, interior trim, cabinetwork, and doors. Ornamental and shade tree. (State tree of Mississippi and State flower of Louisiana.)

62. Sweetbay, *Magnolia virginiana* L. (swampbay, swamp magnolia, laurel magnolia, southern sweetbay, sweetbay magnolia, magnolia). Small to medium-sized tree of Atlantic and Gulf Coastal Plains. Bark brownish gray, smoothish. Leaves shedding in winter or almost evergreen in South, elliptic or narrowly oval, 3–5 in (7.5–13 cm) long, short-pointed, wedge-shaped at base, edges without teeth, thick, shiny bright green and hairless above, whitish and nearly hairless beneath. Flowers cup-shaped, 2–2½ in (5–6 cm) across, white, fragrant. Fruit conelike, 1½–2 (4–5 cm) long and ½ in (1.2 cm) thick, dark red, smooth.

Principal uses: Same as No. 61. Ornamental.

63. Cucumbertree, *Magnolia acuminata* L. (cucumber magnolia, mountain magnolia). Large tree of Appalachian Mountain and Ozark regions and intervening portions of Ohio and Mississippi Valleys; also local in southern Ontario. Bark dark brown, furrowed, with narrow, scaly, forking ridges. Leaves shedding in fall, elliptic or oval, 5–10 in (13–20 cm) long, short-pointed, yellow green and hairless above, light green and soft-hairy or nearly hairless beneath. Flowers bell-shaped, greenish yellow, 2½–3½ in (6–9 cm) long. Fruit conelike, 2–3 in (5–7.5 cm) long and 1 in (2.5 cm) thick, red.

Principal uses: Wood used same as yellow-poplar, No. 60. Ornamental and shade tree.

        nn. Twigs without rings.
          o. Leaves narrow, thick and leathery, evergreen—**Mountain-laurel** (*Kalmia latifolia*).

64. Mountain-laurel, *Kalmia latifolia* L. Evergreen small tree or large shrub of eastern third of United States. Bark thin, dark reddish brown, furrowed into long narrow ridges. Leaves sometimes in pairs or 3's, oblong or elliptic, 3–4 in (7.5–10 cm) long, short-pointed

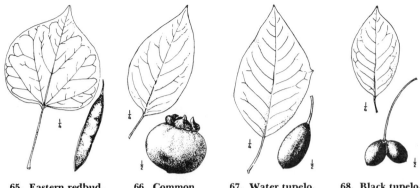

65. Eastern redbud. 66. Common persimmon. 67. Water tupelo. 68. Black tupelo.

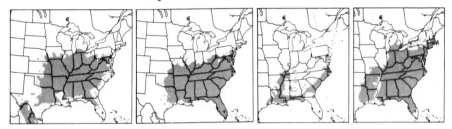

at apex, gradually narrowed at base, not toothed on edges, thick and stiff, dull dark green above, light green beneath, becoming hairless. Flowers numerous, crowded, 1 in (25 mm) across the pinkish saucer-shaped 5-lobed corolla. Fruit a capsule nearly ¼ in (6 mm) in diameter, dark brown, with threadlike style at apex.

Principal uses: Ornamental. Wood for tool handles and turnery. (State flower of Connecticut and Pennsylvania.)

        oo. Leaves mostly broad, thin, shedding in fall.
           p. Leaves rounded, with 5 or 7 main veins from base—**Redbud** (*Cercis*).

65. Eastern redbud, *Cercis canadensis* L. (Judas-tree). Small tree of eastern half of United States and northeastern Mexico. Bark dark brown, furrowed into narrow plates. Leaves rounded, 3–4½ in (7.5–11 cm) long and broad on leafstalk of 1–2 in (2.5–5 cm), short-pointed at apex, base notched or heart-shaped with 5 main veins, edges not toothed, dull green, nearly hairless. Flowers numerous, clustered along twigs in early spring before the leaves, pink, beanlike, ⅜–½ in (10–12 mm) long. Pods 2½–3½ in (6–9 cm) long, and ½ in (1.2 cm) wide, flat, thin, blackish.

Principal use: Ornamental. (State tree of Oklahoma.)

        pp. Leaves mostly oval or elliptic, with 1 main vein.
           q. Leaves broadest below middle—**Persimmon** (*Diospyros*).

66. Common persimmon, *Diospyros virginiana* L. (persimmon). Medium-sized tree of eastern half of United States except northern border. Bark dark brown, thick, deeply divided into small, square, scaly blocks. Leaves oval or elliptic, 2½–6 in (6–15 cm) long, long-pointed, rounded at base, shiny dark green above, pale green and often hairy beneath. Male and female flowers on different trees in spring, ⅜–⅝ in (10–15 mm) long, whitish, at base of leaves. Fruits ¾–1¼ in (2–3 cm) in diameter, yellow or pale orange, maturing in fall, fleshy, sweet, and edible, known as persimmons.

Principal uses: Golf-club heads, shuttles for textile weaving, and veneer in furniture. Sometimes planted for the edible persimmon fruits and for ornament.

        qq. Leaves broadest above middle—**Tupelo** (*Nyssa*).

67. Water tupelo, *Nyssa aquatica* L. (tupelo, tupelo-gum, swamp tupelo, cotton-gum, sour-gum). Large tree with swollen base, swamps of South Atlantic Coastal Plain, Gulf Coastal Plain, and lower Mississippi Valley. Bark dark brown, thin, rough, with scaly ridges. Leaves oval or oblong, 4–6 in (10–15 cm) long, short- or long-pointed, edges often

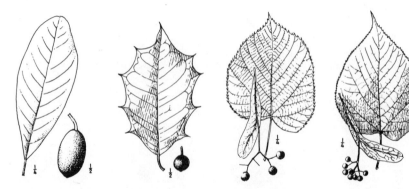

69. Ogeechee tupelo.   **70. American holly.**   **71. American basswood.**   **72. White basswood.**

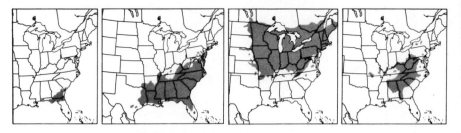

with few teeth, shiny dark green above, pale and soft-hairy beneath. Fruits oblong, 1 in (2.5 cm) long, fleshy, purple, acid, 1-seeded.

Principal uses: Same as No. 68.

68. Black tupelo, blackgum, *Nyssa sylvatica* Marsh. (sour-gum, tupelo, pepperidge, tupelo-gum). Variety: swamp tupelo, *N. sylvatica* var. *biflora* (Walt.) Sarg. (blackgum, swamp blackgum). Large tree of eastern third of United States; also in southern Ontario and Mexico. Bark reddish brown, deeply fissured into irregular and block-shaped ridges. Leaves elliptic or oblong, 2–5 in (5–13 cm) long, short- or blunt-pointed, wedge-shaped or rounded at base, edges not toothed, shiny dark green above, pale and often hairy beneath, turning bright scarlet in fall. Fruits egg-shaped, ⅜–½ in (10–12 mm) long, fleshy, blue black, bitter, 1-seeded.

Principal uses: Furniture, boxes, crates, baskets, and millwork. Pulpwood. Also railroad crossties, bridge ties, and crossing planks. Ornamental and shade tree.

69. Ogeechee tupelo, *Nyssa ogeche* Bartr. (Ogeechee-lime, sour tupelo, sour tupelo-gum, white tupelo, limetree). Small to medium-sized tree, local in swamps of Coastal Plain in South Carolina, Georgia, and Florida. Bark dark brown, thin, irregularly fissured. Leaves elliptic, 4–6 in (10–15 cm) long, short- or blunt-pointed, wedge-shaped at base, edges not toothed, thick, shiny dark green and slightly hairy above, pale and hairy beneath. Fruits 1–1½ in (2.5–4 cm) long, fleshy, red, sour, 1-seeded.

Principal uses: A preserve, Ogeechee-lime, is made from the fruit. The wood is of little importance commercially.

mm. Leaf edges toothed (see also No. 67.)
r. Leaves with few large spiny teeth, thick, evergreen—**Holly** (*Ilex*).

70. American holly, *Ilex opaca* Ait. (white holly, evergreen holly). Medium-sized to large tree of Atlantic coast, Gulf coast, and Mississippi Valley regions. Bark light gray, thin, smoothish, with wartlike projections. Leaves evergreen, elliptic, 2–4 in (5–10 cm) long, spine-pointed and coarsely spiny-toothed, stiff and leathery, shiny green above and yellowish green beneath. Male and female flowers on different trees, small, greenish white. Berry-like fruit round, ¼–⅜ in (6–10 mm) in diameter, red.

Principal uses: Christmas decorations. Specialty items, such as inlays in cabinetmaking and furniture, interior finish fixtures, brush backs, handles, turnery, novelties, wood engravings, woodcuts and carvings, measuring scales and rules for scientific instruments, and parts of musical instruments. Ornamental and shade tree. (State tree of Delaware.)

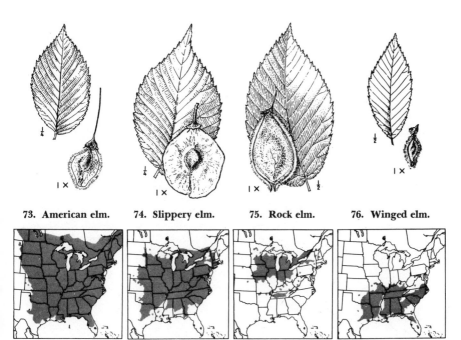

73. American elm. 74. Slippery elm. 75. Rock elm. 76. Winged elm.

 rr. Leaves with many small teeth, thin, shedding in fall.
  s. Leaves with the 2 sides unequal and 1 side larger at base, in 2 rows
   on twig.
   t. Leaves broad, heart-shaped, with leafstalks more than 1¼ in (3
    cm) long (the fragrant, pale yellow flowers and round, nutlike
    fruits borne on strap-shaped greenish stalk)—**Basswood** (or
    linden, *Tilia*).

71. American basswood, *Tilia americana* L. (American linden, linden, linn, beetree, lime-tree; *T. glabra* Vent.). Large tree of northeastern quarter of United States and adjacent Canada. Bark gray, deeply furrowed into narrow, scaly ridges. Leaves in 2 rows, heart-shaped, 4–8 in (10–20 cm) long, long-pointed, coarsely toothed with long-pointed teeth, dark green above, light green beneath with tufts of hair in angles of main veins. Fruits nutlike, ⅜–½ in (10–12 mm) in diameter.
 Principal uses: Boxes (especially food containers), venetian blinds, millwork, furniture, apiary supplies, and woodenware. Also veneer, excelsior, and cooperage. Pulpwood. Shade tree and important honey plant.

72. White basswood, *Tilia heterophylla* Vent. (beetree, linden). Large tree of Appalachian Mountain region west to Mississippi Valley. Bark gray, deeply furrowed. Leaves in 2 rows, heart-shaped 3–6 in (7.5–15 cm) long, long-pointed, the 2 sides unequal at base, finely toothed, shiny dark green and hairless above, beneath white or brownish with dense hairy coat. Fruits nutlike, ¼–⅜ in (6–10 mm) in diameter.
 Principal uses: Same as No. 71.

   tt. Leaves narrower, with leafstalks less than ½ in (1.2 cm) long
    (flowers not on strap-shaped stalk).
    u. Leaves with 1 main vein (midrib) and many parallel side veins;
     fruits flat, elliptic or rounded, bordered with a wing, matur-
     ing in spring (in fall in Nos. 77 and 78)—**Elm** *(Ulmus)*.
     v. Twigs round, not corky winged.

73. American elm, *Ulmus americana* L. (white elm, soft elm, water elm). Large spread-ing tree of eastern half of United States and adjacent Canada, now threatened by the Dutch elm disease. Bark gray, deeply furrowed, with broad, forking, scaly ridges. Twigs soft-hairy, becoming hairless, not corky winged. Leaves in 2 rows, elliptic, 3–6 in (7.5–15 cm) long, long-pointed, the 2 sides unequal, coarsely and doubly toothed with unequal teeth, thin, dark green and smooth or slightly rough above, pale and usually soft-hairy beneath. Fruit elliptic, flat, ⅜–½ in (10–12 mm) long.

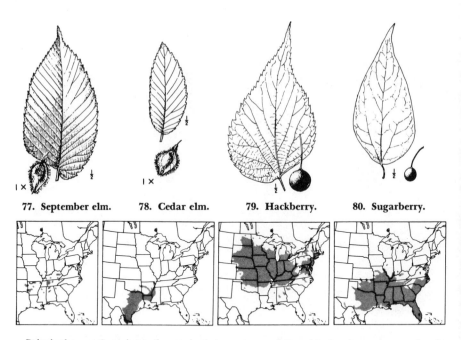

77. September elm.   78. Cedar elm.   79. Hackberry.   80. Sugarberry.

Principal uses: Containers (boxes, baskets, crates, and barrels), furniture, veneer, paneling, toys, novelties, bending stock, and caskets. Shade tree (no longer recommended). Shelterbelts. (State tree of Massachusetts, Nebraska, and North Dakota.)

74. Slippery elm, *Ulmus rubra* Muhl. (red elm, soft elm, gray elm; *U. fulva* Michx.). Medium-sized tree of eastern half of United States and adjacent Canada. Bark dark brown, deeply furrowed, inner bark mucilaginous. Twigs hairy and rough, not corky winged. Leaves in 2 rows, elliptic, 4–8 in (10–20 cm) long, long-pointed, the 2 sides unequal, coarsely and doubly toothed with unequal teeth, thick, dark green and very rough above, densely soft-hairy beneath. Fruit rounded flat, ½–¾ in (12–20 mm) long.
Principal uses: Wood used same as No. 73.

vv. Twigs usually becoming corky winged.

75. Rock elm, *Ulmus thomasii* Sarg. (cork elm, hickory elm; *U. racemosa* Thomas, not Borkh.). Medium-sized to large tree of northeastern quarter of United States and adjacent Canada. Bark gray, deeply furrowed. Twigs often corky winged. Leaves in 2 rows, elliptic, 2–4 in (5–10 cm) long, short-pointed, the 2 sides unequal, coarsely and doubly toothed with unequal teeth, thick, shiny dark green and smooth above, pale and soft-hairy beneath. Fruit elliptic, flat, ⅝–¾ in (15–20 mm) long.
Principal uses: Wood used same as No. 73. Shade tree.

76. Winged elm, *Ulmus alata* Michx. (wahoo, cork elm). Medium-sized to large tree of southeastern quarter of United States. Bark light brown, thin, irregularly fissured. Twigs usually becoming corky winged. Leaves in 2 rows, oblong 1¼–2½ in (3–6 cm) long, short-pointed, the 2 sides unequal, coarsely and doubly toothed with unequal teeth, thick, dark green and smooth above, pale and soft-hairy beneath. Fruit elliptic, flat, ⅜ in (10 mm) long.
Principal uses: Wood used same as No. 73. Shade tree.

77. September elm, *Ulmus serotina* Sarg. (red elm). Medium-sized tree of Mississippi Valley region from Kentucky to Georgia and Oklahoma. Bark light brown, thin, fissured. Twigs often corky winged. Leaves in 2 rows, oblong, 2–3 in (5–7.5 cm) long, long-pointed, the 2 sides unequal, coarsely and doubly toothed with unequal teeth, shiny yellow green and smooth above, pale and slightly hairy beneath. Flowering in fall. Fruit elliptic, ½ in (12 mm) long, flat.
Principal uses: Wood used same as No. 73.

78. Cedar elm, *Ulmus crassifolia* Nutt. (basket elm, red elm, southern rock elm). Large tree of lower Mississippi Valley to Texas and adjacent Mexico. Bark light brown, fissured. Twigs usually becoming corky winged. Leaves in 2 rows, elliptic, 1–2 in (2.5–5 cm) long,

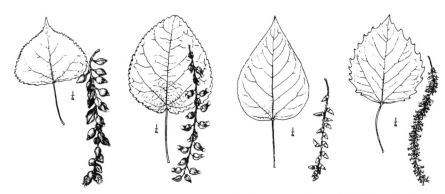

81. Eastern cotton-   **82. Swamp cotton-**   **83. Balsam poplar.**   **84. Bigtooth aspen.**
wood   **wood.**

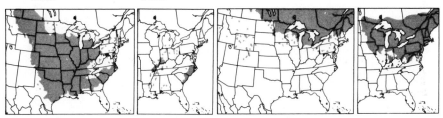

short-pointed or rounded, the 2 sides unequal, coarsely and doubly toothed with unequal teeth, thick, shiny dark green and rough above, soft-hairy beneath. Flowering in late summer or fall. Fruit oblong, ⅜–½ in (10–12 mm) long, flat.

Principal uses: Wood used same as No. 73.

uu. Leaves with 3 main veins from base; fruits round, wingless, maturing in fall—**Hackberry** (*Celtis*).

79. Hackberry, *Celtis occidentalis* L. (sugarberry, nettletree, false-elm, beaverwood, common hackberry). Medium-sized to large tree of eastern half of United States except southern border; also in adjacent Canada. Bark light brown to gray, with corky warts or ridges becoming scaly. Leaves in 2 rows, oval, 2–4¼ in (5–11 cm) long, usually long-pointed, the 2 sides unequal, sharply toothed except in lower part, with 3 main veins from base, bright green and smooth or sometimes rough above, paler and nearly hairless beneath. Fruits ¼–⅜ in (6–10 mm) in diameter, dark purple, 1-seeded.

Principal uses: Same as No. 80. Shelterbelts and shade tree.

80. Sugarberry, *Celtis laevigata* Willd. (sugar hackberry, hackberry, Texas sugarberry, southern hackberry; *C. mississippiensis* Spach). Medium-sized to large tree of southeastern quarter of United States, with a variety west to New Mexico and northeastern Mexico. Bark gray, smoothish, with prominent corky warts. Leaves in 2 rows, broadly lance-shaped, 1½–4 in (4–10 cm) long, long-pointed, the 2 sides unequal edges smooth or sometimes with a few teeth, with 3 main veins from base, dark green and usually smooth above, paler and usually hairless beneath. Fruits ¼ in (6 mm) in diameter, orange red or purple, 1-seeded.

Principal uses: Furniture, millwork, and sporting and athletic goods. Also boxes and crates and plywood. Shelterbelts and shade tree.

ss. Leaves with both sides equal, spreading around twig (in 2 rows in No. 97).

w. Leafstalks more than 1½ in (4 cm) long, slender; seeds cottony, capsules in long clusters—**Cottonwood, poplar** (*Populus*; see also No. 164).

81. Eastern cottonwood, *Populus deltoides* Bartr. ex. Marsh. (southern cottonwood, eastern poplar, Carolina poplar, necklace poplar, álamo; *P. balsamifera* auth.). Variety: plains cottonwood, var. *occidentalis* Rydb. (plains poplar, Texas cottonwood; *P. sargentii* Dode). Large tree of eastern half of United States and adjacent Canada. Bark at first yellowish green and smooth, becoming gray and deeply furrowed. Leaves triangular, 3–6 in (7.5–15 cm) long and wide, long-pointed, coarsely toothed with curved teeth, hairless, light green and shiny (broader with larger teeth in plains cottonwood). Leafstalks flat.

Principal uses: Boxes and crates, especially food containers; interior parts of furniture, interior trim; plywood, agricultural implements; woodenware including cutting boards and meat boards; matches. Pulpwood. Shade tree and shelterbelts. (Cottonwood, *Populus* spp., is the State tree of Kansas. Cottonwood, *P. sargentii*, is the State tree of Wyoming.)

82. Swamp cottonwood, *Populus heterophylla* L. (swamp poplar, black cottonwood, river cottonwood, downy poplar). Medium-sized to large tree of Atlantic coast, Gulf coast, and Mississippi Valley regions. Bark grayish brown, furrowed into scaly ridges. Leaves heart-shaped, 4–7 in (10–18 cm) long and nearly as wide, short-pointed or rounded at apex, finely toothed with small, curved teeth, hairy when unfolding but becoming smooth or remaining woolly beneath, dark green above, paler beneath. Leafstalks round.

Principal uses: Wood used same as No. 81.

83. Balsam poplar, *Populus balsamifera* L. (balm, balm-of-Gilead, bam, tacamahac, hackmatack, cottonwood; *P. tacamahacca* Mill.). Large tree widely distributed in northeastern border of United States, northern Rocky Mountain region, and across Canada to Alaska. Bark at first reddish brown and smooth, becoming gray, furrowed, with flat, scaly ridges. Winter buds resinous and fragrant. Leaves oval or broadly lance-shaped, 3–5 in (7.5–13 cm) long, short-pointed, finely toothed with rounded teeth, hairless or nearly so, shiny dark green above, pale green beneath. Leafstalks round.

Principal uses: Boxes and crates. Pulpwood. Balm-of-Gilead, derived from the buds, is used in cough medicine. Ornamental.

84. Bigtooth aspen, *Populus grandidentata* Michx. (largetooth aspen, poplar, popple). Medium-sized tree of northeastern quarter of United States and adjacent Canada. Bark greenish, smooth, thin, becoming dark brown, irregularly fissured, with flat ridges. Leaves elliptic or nearly round, 2½–4 in (6–10 cm) long, coarsely toothed with curved teeth, hairless, dark green above, paler beneath. Leafstalks flattened.

Principal uses: Same as No. 164.

> ww. Leafstalks less than 1 in (2.5 cm) long; seeds not hairy (except Nos. 92 and 93).
> x. Leaf edges with teeth of 2 sizes and slightly irregular.
> y. Fruit a cone.
> z. Fruit with many scales and nutlets; bark of papery layers, peeling off—**Birch** (*Betula*).
> A. Leaves mostly with 9–11 veins on each side; cones upright.

85. Yellow birch, *Betula alleghaniensis* Britton (gray birch, silver birch, swamp birch; *B. lutea* Michx. f.). Large tree of Northeastern United States and adjacent Canada and Appalachian Mountain region. Bark aromatic on young branches, yellowish or silvery gray, shiny, separating into papery, curly strips; on old trunks reddish brown. Leaves oval, 3–5 in (7.5–13 cm) long, long- or short-pointed, sharply and doubly toothed, mostly with 9–11 main veins on each side, nearly hairless, dull dark green above, yellow green below. Cones ¾–1¼ in (2–3 cm) long.

Principal uses: Lumber and veneer for furniture (one of the principal woods), cabinets, boxes, woodenware, handles, and millwork such as interior finish and flush doors; small turned products and barrel staves. One of the principal woods for distillation products, such as wood alcohol. Pulpwood, fuelwood, charcoal. Shade tree.

86. Sweet birch, *Betula lenta* L. (black birch, cherry birch). Medium-sized to large tree of Appalachian Mountain region and adjacent Canada. Bark aromatic on young branches, dark reddish brown, smooth, shiny; on large trunks fissured into scaly plates. Leaves oval, 2½–5 in (6–10 cm) long, long-pointed, sharply and doubly toothed, mostly with 9–11 veins on each side, silky-hairy beneath when young but becoming nearly hairless, dark dull green above, light yellow green beneath. Cones ¾–1½ in (2–4 cm) long.

Principal uses: Same as No. 85. Birch oil (from bark).

> AA. Leaves mostly with 4–9 veins on each side; cones hanging down (upright in No. 87).

87. River birch, *Betula nigra* L. (red birch, black birch, water birch). Medium-sized to large tree of wet soil in eastern half of United States (the only birch at low altitudes in Southeast). Bark reddish brown or silvery gray, shiny, becoming fissured and separating into papery scales. Leaves oval, 1½–3 in (4–7.5 cm) long, short-pointed, wedge-shaped at base, doubly toothed, mostly with 7–9 veins on each side, shiny dark green above, whitish and usually hairy beneath. Cones 1–1½ in (2.5–4 cm) long.

Principal uses: Ornamental and erosion control.

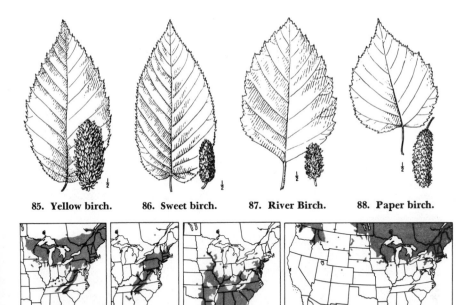

85. Yellow birch.   **86. Sweet birch.**   **87. River Birch.**   **88. Paper birch.**

88. Paper birch, *Betula papyrifera* Marsh. (canoe birch, white birch, silver birch). Medium-sized to large tree, including its varieties widely distributed in northeastern border of United States, northern Rocky Mountain region, and across Canada to Alaska. Bark white, smooth, thin, separating into papery strips. Leaves oval, 2–4 in (5–10 cm) long, long-pointed, wedge-shaped or rounded at base, coarsely and doubly toothed, mostly with 5–9 veins on each side dull dark green and hairless above, light yellow green and smooth or slightly hairy beneath. Cones narrow, 1½–2 in (4–5 cm) long and ⅜ in (1 cm) wide, slender-stalked and hanging down.

Principal uses: Specialty veneer products including ice cream sticks, picnic spoons, tongue depressors, and toothpicks. Small turned or rived products, including bobbins, clothespins, spools, broom handles, dowels, and toys. Pulpwood. Fuelwood, especially fireplace wood. Bark used by Indians for canoes and small articles. Ornamental and shade tree. (State tree of New Hampshire.)

89. Gray birch, *Betula populifolia* Marsh. (white birch, wire birch). Small tree of northeastern United States and adjacent Canada. Bark grayish white, smooth, thin; on larger trunks darker and fissured. Leaves triangular, 2–3 in (5–7.5 cm) long, long-pointed, sharply and doubly toothed, mostly with 4–8 veins on each side, dark green and shiny above, paler beneath. Cones ¾–1 in (2–2.5 cm) long, slender-stalked and hanging down.

Principal uses: Spools and other turned articles. Fuelwood.

> zz. Fruit with many papery scales enclosing nutlets; bark finely fissured—**Hophornbeam** (*Ostrya*).

90. Eastern hophornbeam, *Ostrya virginiana* (Mill.) K. Koch (American hophornbeam, hornbeam, "ironwood"). Small to medium-sized tree of eastern half of United States, also in mountains of Mexico and Guatemala. Bark light brown, fissured into narrow flat scales. Leaves ovate, 2½–4½ in (6–11 cm) long, long-pointed at apex and slightly notched at base, sharply and doubly toothed, above dull yellow green and hairless, beneath paler with tufts of hairs along midvein, turning yellow in autumn. Fruit clusters conelike, 1½ in (4 cm) long, composed of nutlets ⅜ in (1 cm) long, each within a light brown papery flattened scale.

Principal uses: Tool handles, small wooden articles, fenceposts.

> yy. Fruit of few nutlets above leaflike 3-pointed scales; bark dark gray, smooth, on angled (fluted) trunk—**Hornbeam** (*Carpinus*).

29

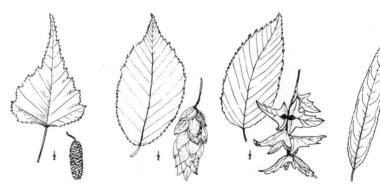

89. Gray birch. **90. Eastern hophorn-beam.** **91. American horn-beam.** **92. Black willow.**

91. American hornbeam, *Carpinus caroliniana* Walt. (blue-beech, water-beech). Small tree of eastern half of United States, also south in mountains from Mexico to Honduras. Bark dark gray, smooth, the trunk angled (fluted) with vertical ridges. Leaves ovate, 2½–4½ in (6–11 cm) long, long-pointed at apex and rounded at base, sharply and doubly toothed, above dull blue green and hairless, beneath paler with tufts of hairs along veins, turning scarlet and orange in autumn. Fruit clusters 2–4 in (5–10 cm) long, with few nutlets ⅜ in (1 cm) long at base of leaflike 3-pointed toothed scales about 1 in (2.5 cm) long.

Principal uses: Tool handles, small wooden articles. Ornamental.

xx. Leaf edges with uniform teeth.
    B. Leaves finely toothed, with curved side veins.
        c. Leaves narrow, more than 3 times as long as wide (seeds hairy, capsules in long clusters)—**Willow** (*Salix*).

92. Black willow, *Salix nigra* Marsh. (swamp willow, western black willow; *S. gooddingii* Ball). Medium-sized to large tree of wet soil, Eastern and Southwestern United States and adjacent Canada and Mexico. Bark dark brown or blackish, deeply furrowed, with scaly, forking ridges. Leaves lance-shaped, 2½–5 in (6–13 cm) long, long-pointed, finely toothed, green on both surfaces, shiny above and pale beneath, hairless or nearly so. Male and female flowers on different trees in early spring, minute, yellowish or greenish, many in narrow clusters 1½–3 in (4–7.5 cm) long.

Principal uses: Millwork, household furniture, signs, boxes. Also doors, veneer panels, cabinetwork, toys, cutting boards, picture frames, slack cooperage, excelsior, charcoal, woodenware, and artifical limbs. Wood carvings. Pulpwood. Erosion control, including poles in mats for stabilization of river banks. A honey plant. Shade tree.

93. Peachleaf willow, *Salix amygdaloides* Anderss. (almond willow, peach willow, Wright willow). Small to medium-sized tree of wet soil, nearly across Northern United States and adjacent Canada, south to Texas and Arizona and adjacent Mexico. Bark brown, irregularly fissured into flat ridges. Leaves lance-shaped, 2½–5 in (6–13 cm) long, long-pointed, finely toothed, shiny green above and pale beneath, hairless. Male and female flowers on different trees in early spring, minute, yellowish or greenish, many in narrow clusters 2–3 in (5–7½ cm) long.

Principal uses: Same as no. 92.

cc. Leaves less than 3 times as long as wide.
    DD. Leafstalks without glands; fruit 4-winged—**Silverbell** (*Halesia*).

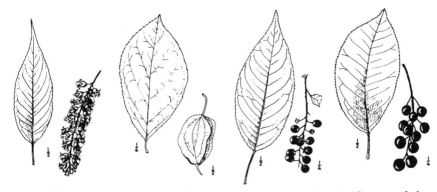

**93. Peachleaf willow.   94. Carolina silver-   95. Black cherry.   96. Common choke-
bell.   cherry.**

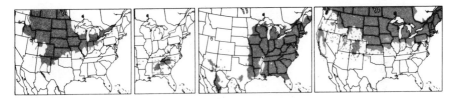

94. Carolina silverbell, *Halesia carolina* L. (oppossum-wood, snowdroptree, mountain silverbell). Medium-sized to large tree of Southeastern United States. Bark reddish brown, separating into scales or plates. Leaves elliptic, 3–6 in (7.5–15 cm) long, long-pointed at apex, wedge-shaped or rounded at base, finely toothed, dull dark green and hairless above, beneath paler and often hairy on veins, turning yellow in autumn. Flowers bell-shaped, white, ½–2 in (1.2–5 cm) long, 4-lobed. Fruit oblong, 1½–2 in (4–5 cm) long, 4-winged, 1-seeded.

Principal uses: Lumber. Ornament, shade.

> DD. Leafstalks usually with 2 dotlike glands near blade;
> fruit a small cherry—**Cherry, plum** (*Prunus*).

95. Black cherry, *Prunus serotina* Ehrh. (wild black cherry, rum cherry, mountain black cherry, wild cherry). Medium-sized to large tree of eastern half of United States and adjacent Canada, with varieties in Southwest and Mexico. Bark dark reddish brown, smooth at first, becoming irregularly fissured and scaly. Leaves elliptic, 2–5 in long (5–13 cm), long-pointed, finely toothed, shiny dark green above, light green and often slightly hairy beneath. Flowers white, ¼ in (6 mm) long, in spring. Fruits edible cherries ⅜ in (10 mm) in diameter, black.

Principal uses: Furniture; printers' blocks for mounting electrotype plates; solid and veneer paneling, patterns, professional and scientific instruments, piano actions, handles, woodenware, toys. Wild cherry syrup (from bark) for cough medicine. Edible wild cherries, used for jelly and wine. Shade tree.

96. Common chokecherry, *Prunus virginiana* L. (black chokecherry, eastern chokecherry, Western chokecherry, California chokecherry; *P. demissa* (Nutt.) D. Dietr., *P. melanocarpa* (A Nels.) Rydb.). Thicket-forming shrub or small tree widespread across United States. Bark smooth, brown or gray, becoming furrowed and scaly. Leaves elliptic to obovate, 2–4 in (5–10 cm) long, abruptly short-pointed at apex, edges sharply saw-toothed, thick, above shiny dark green, beneath paler and sometimes slightly hairy. Flowers many along a stalk, white, ⅜–½ in (10–12 mm) wide. Fruits edible chokecherries ¼–⅜ in (6–10 mm) in diameter, dark red or blackish.

Principal uses: Fruits edible, astringent when raw, used in making some wines and jelly, also wildlife food.

> BB. Leaves coarsely toothed, with straight, parallel side veins;
> fruit a spiny bur with edible nuts.
> E. Leaves about twice as long as wide—**Beech** (*Fagus*).

31

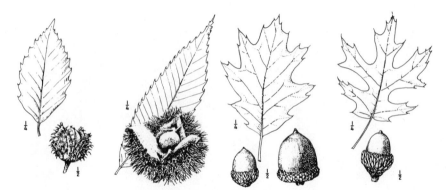

97. American beech. **98. American chest- 99. Northern red oak.** **100. Scarlet oak.**
nut.

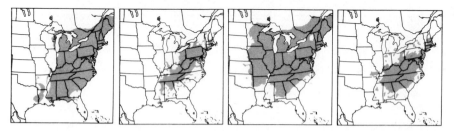

97. American beech, *Fagus grandifolia* Ehrh. (beech). Large tree of eastern third of United States and adjacent Canada, also a variety local in mountains of eastern Mexico. Bark blue gray, thin, smooth. Leaves in 2 rows, oval, 2½–5 in (6–13 cm) long, long-pointed, coarsely toothed, the side veins parallel, dark blue green above and light green beneath, hairless or nearly so. Fruit a shiny bur ¾ in (2 cm) long, containing 2 or 3 triangular, edible nuts ½–¾ in (12–20 mm) long, known as beechnuts.

Principal uses: Boxes (especially food containers), baskets, and pallets; furniture (particularly chairs), flooring, sash, doors, trim, paneling, and general millwork; woodenware and novelties; and handles brooms, and brushes. Railroad crossties. Pulpwood. Distillation products, charcoal, and fireplace wood. Beechnuts. Shade tree.

EE. Leaves more than 3 times as long as wide—**Chestnut** (*Castanea*).

98. American chestnut, *Castanea dentata* (Marsh.) Borkh. (chestnut). Sprouts persisting from roots, formerly large tree (killed by chestnut blight disease), of Appalachian Mountain and Ohio Valley regions; also in extreme southern Ontario. Now almost exterminated by chestnut blight, but root sprouts sometimes bear chestnuts before dying. Bark dark brown, irregularly fissured into broad, flat ridges. Leaves narrowly oblong, 5–9 in (13–23 cm) long, and 1½–3 in (4–7.5 cm) wide, long-pointed, coarsely toothed with slightly curved teeth, many parallel side veins, yellow green, hairless. Fruit a spiny bur 2–2½ in (5–6 cm) in diameter, containing 2 or 3 broad, flattened, edible chestnuts ½–1 in (12–25 mm) wide.

Principal uses: Formerly, the wood was the main domestic source of tannin. Formerly, general construction, furniture, caskets, boxes and crates; plywood, poles, railroad crossties, pulpwood. Fuelwood. Edible chestnuts. The leaves are an official drug.

ii (i on p. 20). Winter buds 3 or more in cluster at tip of twig; pith of twigs star-shaped in cross section; fruit an acorn—**Oak** (*Quercus*).

Most of the 22 species of eastern oaks included here have commercially important woods, which are grouped into red oaks and white oaks.

Principal uses: Oaks are the most important hardwood timbers in the United States and first in sawtimber volume. However, demands have been changing. The greatest single use is for hardwood dimension and flooring (oak is the principal flooring wood). Oak is popular for household and public furniture. Uses as veneer and plywood in millwork and furniture are increasing. The leading wood for railroad crossties and an important source of mine timbers. White oak is outstanding for tight barrels, kegs, and casks for storing and

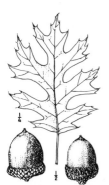

| 101. Shumard oak. | 102. Pin oak. | 103. Northern pin oak. | 104. Nuttall oak. |

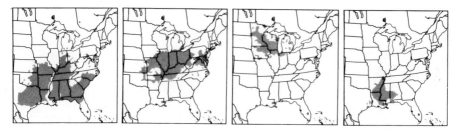

curing whiskey and wine. Truck and trailer beds, containers, pallets, caskets, boxes, paneling, jigs, and shipbuilding and boatbuilding. Pulpwood, fenceposts, piling, fuelwood and charcoal. Some species are important shade trees. The acorns are eaten by wildlife and livestock. ("Native oak" *Quercus* spp., is the State tree of Illinois. Oak, *Quercus* spp., is the State tree of Iowa.)

> F. Leaves and their lobes, if present, bristle-tipped; acorns maturing in second-year—**Black oaks** (or red oaks, the lumber of most species included here usually sold as red oak).
> G. Leaves broad, more than 2 in (5 cm) wide, margins distinctly lobed and with bristle-pointed teeth.
> H. Under surface of leaves green and nearly hairless.

99. Northern red oak, *Quercus rubra* L. (red oak, common red oak, gray oak, eastern red oak, mountain red .oak; *Q. borealis* Michx. f.). Large tree of eastern half of United States (except southern border) and in adjacent Canada. Bark dark brown, fissured into broad, flat ridges. Leaves elliptic, 5–9 in (13–23 cm) long, 7–11-lobed less than halfway to middle, the lobes with a few irregular bristle-pointed teeth, dull dark green above, beneath pale yellow green, hairless or nearly so, usually turning red in fall. Acorns ⅝–1⅛ in (15–28 mm) long, with deep or shallow cup.
Principal uses: The most important lumber tree of red oak group. Shade tree. (State tree of New Jersey.)

100. Scarlet oak, *Quercus coccinea* Muenchh. (Spanish oak, red oak, black oak). Large tree of eastern third of United States except southern border. Bark dark brown or gray, fissured into irregular, scaly ridges. Leaves elliptic, 3–6 in (7.5–15 cm) long, deeply 7-lobed nearly to middle, lobes broader toward tip and with few bristle-pointed teeth, edges rounded between lobes, bright green, shiny, and hairless above, paler and nearly hairless beneath, turning scarlet in fall. Acorns ½–¾ in (12–20 mm) long, a third to half enclosed by the deep cup.
Principal uses: Red oak lumber. Shade tree. (Official tree of District of Columbia.)

101. Shumard oak, *Quercus shumardii* Buckl. (Shumard red oak, southern red oak, swamp red oak, red oak, spotted oak). Large tree of Eastern United States, chiefly in Atlantic coast, Gulf coast, and Mississippi Valley regions. Bark gray or reddish brown, fissured into scaly plates. Leaves elliptic, 3–7 in (7.5–18 cm) long, 5–9 lobed more than halfway to middle, lobes with few bristle-pointed teeth, edges rounded or pointed between

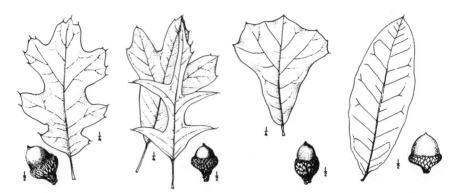

105. Black oak.   106. Southern red oak. 107. Blackjack oak.   108. Shingle oak.

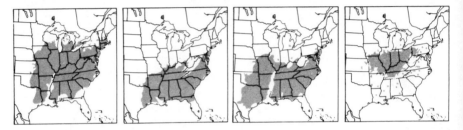

the lobes, dark green and shiny above, beneath light green with tufts of hairs along midvein. Acorns ⅝–1⅛ in (15–28 mm) long, with shallow or deep cup.
Principal uses: Red oak lumber. Shade tree.

102. Pin oak, *Quercus palustris* Muenchh. (swamp oak). Large tree of northeastern quarter of United States except northern border; also in southern Ontario. Bark grayish brown, smooth, becoming fissured with low, scaly ridges. Leaves elliptic, 3–5 in (7.5–13 cm) long, deeply 5–7-lobed nearly to middle, lobes with few bristle-pointed teeth, dark green and very shiny above, light green and nearly hairless beneath. Acorns rounded, about ½ in (12 mm) in diameter, with shallow cup.
Principal uses: Red oak lumber. Piling. Shade tree.

103. Northern pin oak, *Quercus ellipsoidalis* E. J. Hill (jack oak, Hills oak, black oak). Medium-sized to large tree of north central United States. Bark gray brown, smoothish, becoming fissured into thin plates. Leaves elliptic, 3–5 in (7.5–13 cm) long, deeply 5–7-lobed with bristle-pointed teeth, shiny green above, paler beneath, hairless except for tufts of hairs along midvein beneath. Acorns elliptic or rounded, ½–¾ in (12–20 mm) long, a third to half enclosed by deep cup.
Principal use: Red oak lumber.

104. Nuttall oak, *Quercus nuttallii* Palmer. Large tree of lower Mississippi Valley and Gulf Coastal Plain regions from Alabama to Missouri and Texas. Bark dark brownish gray, slightly fissured. Leaves oblong or elliptic, 4–8 in (10–20 cm) long, deeply 5- or 7-lobed, the narrow lobes with few bristle-pointed teeth, dark green above, paler and nearly hairless beneath. Acorns oblong, ¾–1¼ in (20–30 mm) long, a third to half enclosed by deep cup.
Principal uses: Red oak lumber. Furniture, truck-trailer flooring, railroad car decks, pallets, cabinetwork, interior trim, specialties.

HH. Under surface of leaves with brownish or gray hairy coat.

105. Black oak, *Quercus velutina* Lam. (yellow oak, quercitron oak). Large tree of eastern half of United States and southern Ontario. Bark blackish, thick, deeply furrowed, with blocklike ridges; inner bark yellow. Leaves elliptic, 4–10 in (10–25 cm) long, 7–9-lobed about halfway to middle, lobes broad and with few bristle-pointed teeth, shiny dark green above, usually brown-hairy beneath, turning dull red or brown in fall. Acorns ⅝–¾ in (15–20 mm) long, half enclosed by deep cup.
Principal uses: Red oak lumber. Bark formerly was a source of tannin and yellow dye. Shade tree.

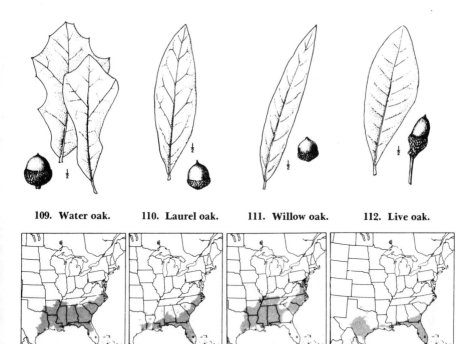

109. Water oak.   **110. Laurel oak.**   **111. Willow oak.**   **112. Live oak.**

106. Southern red oak, *Quercus falcata* Michx. (Spanish oak, water oak, red oak; *Q. rubra* auth.) Variety: cherrybark oak, swamp red oak, var. *pagodaefolia* Ell. Large tree of Atlantic coast, Gulf coast, and Mississippi Valley regions. Bark dark brown, thick, fissured into narrow ridges. Leaves elliptic or slightly triangular, 3–8 in long, (7.5–20 cm) deeply 3–7-lobed nearly to middle or slightly 3-lobed near broad apex (less deeply 5–11-lobed in cherry-bark oak), lobes with 1–3 bristle-pointed teeth, dark green hairless, and shiny above, densely rusty or grayish hairy beneath, turning brown or orange in fall. Acorns rounded, about ½ in (12 mm) in diameter, with shallow cup.
Principal uses: Red oak lumber. Shade tree.

107. Blackjack oak, *Quercus marilandica* Muenchh. (blackjack, jack oak, black oak, barren oak). Small tree of eastern half of United States except northern border. Bark blackish, thick and rough, divided into small squarish blocks. Leaves slightly triangular, 3–7 in (7.5–18 cm) long, broadest at 3-lobed apex, gradually narrowed to rounded base, the broad lobes with 1 or few bristle-pointed teeth, dark green, hairless, and shiny above, brownish or rusty-hairy beneath, turning brown or yellow in fall. Acorns ¾ in (20 mm) long, about half enclosed by deep cup.
Principal uses: Railroad crossties, fuelwood, charcoal.

        GG. Leaves narrow, less than 2 in (5 cm) broad, with edges straight or slightly 3-lobed.

108. Shingle oak, *Quercus imbricaria* Michx. (laurel oak). Medium-sized or large tree of eastern third of United States (except extreme north and south). Bark smooth, light brown, becoming fissured into brown scaly ridges. Leaves oblong, or lance-shaped, 3–6 in (7.5–13 cm) long, short-pointed or rounded at both ends, edges slightly wavy, shiny dark green and hairless above, pale green and hairy beneath. Acorns rounded, ½–⅝ in (12–15 mm) long, a third to half enclosed by deep cup.
Principal uses: Red oak lumber, shingles.

109. Water oak, *Quercus nigra* L. (possum oak, spotted oak). Large tree of Atlantic coast, Gulf coast, and Mississippi Valley regions. Bark gray, fissured into irregular, scaly ridges. Leaves oblong, 1½–5 in (4–13 cm) long, broadest at rounded or 3-lobed apex or sometimes with several lobes, dull blue green, paler beneath with tufts ot hairs along vein angles, turning yellow in fall and shedding in winter. Acorns rounded, ⅜–⅝ in (10–15 mm) in diameter, with shallow cup.
Principal uses: Red oak lumber. Shade tree.

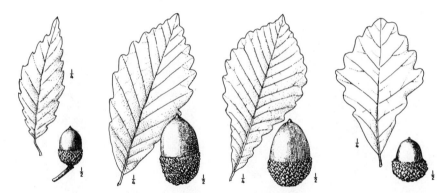

| 113. Chinkapin oak. | 114. Chestnut oak. | 115. Swamp chestnut oak. | 116. Swamp white oak. |

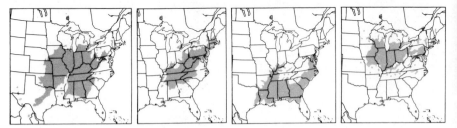

110. Laurel oak, *Quercus laurifolia* Michx. (Darlington oak, water oak, diamondleaf oak). Large tree of South Atlantic and Gulf Coastal Plains. Bark dark brown, smoothish, on large trunks becoming deeply furrowed, with broad ridges. Leaves narrowly oblong, 2–5½ in (5–14 cm) long, short-pointed, edges not toothed or lobed, shiny dark green above, light green beneath, hairless, nearly evergreen but shedding in early spring. Acorns rounded, about ½ in (12 mm) in diameter, with shallow cup.
Principal uses: Red oak lumber. Shade tree.

111. Willow oak, *Quercus phellos* L. (peach oak, pin oak, swamp willow oak). Large tree of Atlantic coast, Gulf coast, and Mississippi Valley regions. Bark gray or brown, smoothish, on large trunks becoming fissured into scaly ridges. Leaves very narrowly oblong or lance-shaped, 2–4 in (5–10 cm) long and ⅜–¾ in (1–2 cm) broad, short-pointed with straight or slightly wavy edges, light green and shiny above, beneath dull and slightly hairy or nearly hairless, turning pale yellow in fall. Acorns small, rounded, ⅜ in (10 mm) in diameter, with shallow cup.
Principal uses: Red oak lumber. Shade tree.

        FF. Leaves and their lobes not bristle-tipped; acorns maturing in first year
          —**White oaks** (lumber of most species sold as white oak).
          I. Leaves with edges usually straight and rolled under, evergreen.

112. Live oak, *Quercus virginiana* Mill. (sand live oak). Medium-sized, widespreading tree of South Atlantic coast and Gulf coast regions. Bark dark brown, furrowed and slightly scaly. Leaves evergreen, elliptic or oblong, 2–5 in (5–13 cm) long, usually rounded at apex, edges usually straight and rolled under, shiny dark green above, whitish hairy beneath. Acorns 1–5 on stalks ½–3 in (1.2–7.5 cm) long, ¾–1 in (20–25 mm) long, narrow, with deep cup.
Principal uses: Shade tree. Formerly used in shipbuilding. (State tree of Georgia.)

          II. Leaves with edges lobed or toothed, shedding in fall.
          J. Leaf edges wavy with uniform, rounded teeth (**Chestnut oaks**).

113. Chinkapin oak, *Quercus muehlenbergii* Engelm. (chestnut oak, yellow chestnut oak, rock chestnut oak, yellow oak). Large tree of eastern half of United States and local in New Mexico; also in southern Ontario. Bark light gray, thin, fissured, and flaky. Leaves narrowly elliptic or broadly lance-shaped, 4–6 in (10–15 cm) long, short- or long-pointed, usually rounded at base, edges wavy with coarse, slightly curved teeth, dark or yellowish green above, whitish hairy beneath, turning orange and scarlet in fall. Acorns ½–¾ in (12–20 mm)

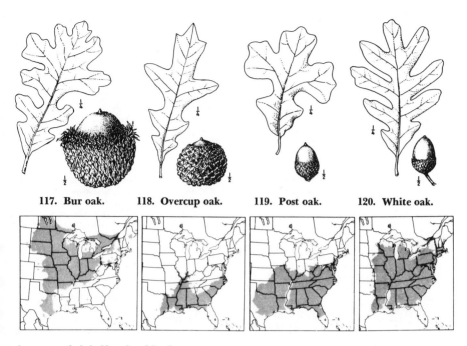

117. Bur oak.   **118. Overcup oak.**   **119. Post oak.**   **120. White oak.**

long, rounded, half enclosed by deep cup.
Principal use: White oak lumber.

114. Chestnut oak, *Quercus prinus* L. (rock chestnut oak, rock oak, tanbark oak; *Q. montana* Willd.). Large tree of Appalachian Mountain and Ohio Valley regions; also in southern Ontario. Bark brown or blackish, on large trunks becoming deeply furrowed into broad ridges. Leaves elliptic or obovate, 5–8 in (13–20 cm) long, short- or long-pointed at apex and base, edges wavy with rounded teeth, shiny yellow green above, paler and hairy or nearly hairless beneath, turning dull orange in fall. Acorns large, 1–1½ in (25–38 mm) long, a third to half enclosed by thin, deep, warty cup.
Principal uses: White oak lumber. Furniture, flooring, and cooperage. The bark formerly was a source of tannin.

115. Swamp chestnut oak, *Quercus michauxii* Nutt. (cow oak, basket oak; *Q. prinus* L., in part). Large tree of Atlantic coast, Gulf coast, and Mississippi Valley regions. Bark light gray, fissured and scaly. Leaves obovate or elliptic, 4–8 in (10–20 cm) long, gradually narrowed toward base, usually broadest above middle, edges wavy with rounded teeth, shiny dark green above, densely grayish hairy beneath, turning crimson in fall. Acorns large, 1–1½ in (25–38 mm) long, a third or more enclosed by thick, deep cup composed of many distinct scales.
Principal use: White oak lumber.

116. Swamp white oak, *Quercus bicolor* Willd. (white oak). Large tree of northeastern quarter of United States and adjacent Canada. Bark brown, scaly, on old trunks becoming furrowed into long, scaly ridges. Leaves obovate, 4–6 in (10–15 cm) long, gradually narrowed toward base, broadest above middle, edges wavy with rounded teeth or lobes, dark green and shiny above, densely whitish hairy beneath, turning yellow brown, orange, or red in fall. Acorns usually in pairs on stalks 1½–3 in (4–7.5 cm) long, ¾–1¼ in (20–31 mm) long, a third enclosed by deep cup.
Principal uses: White oak lumber. Railroad crossties, pallets, flooring, and cooperage.

JJ. Leaf edges deeply lobed.

117. Bur oak, *Quercus macrocarpa* Michx. (mossycup oak, blue oak). Large tree of eastern half of United States west to Montana and in adjacent Canada west to Saskatchewan. Bark light brown, deeply furrowed into scaly ridges. Leaves obovate, 4–10 in (10–25 cm) long, wedge-shaped at base, broadest above middle, lower part deeply lobed nearly to middle and the upper half with shallow lobes, dark green and usually shiny above, grayish or whitish hairy beneath, turning yellow or brown in fall. Acorns usually large, ¾–2 in

37

(20–50 mm) long, broad, half enclosed by large cup with fringelike border.
Principal uses: White oak lumber. Shelterbelts. Shade tree and ornamental.

118. Overcup oak, *Quercus lyrata* Walt. (swamp post oak, swamp white oak, water white oak). Medium-sized to large tree of Atlantic coast, Gulf coast, and Mississippi Valley regions. Bark brownish gray, fissured into large irregular, scaly ridges. Leaves narrowly oblong or obovate, 6–8 in (15–20 cm) long, wedge-shaped at base, deeply lobed nearly to middle with 7–9 rounded or pointed lobes, the 2 lowest lobes on each side much smaller, dark green and hairless above, white hairy beneath, turning yellowish, orange, or scarlet in fall. Acorns ½–1 in (12–25 mm) long, nearly enclosed by spherical deep cup with ragged edge.
Principal use: White oak lumber.

119. Post oak, *Quercus stellata* Wangenh. (iron oak). Variety: Delta post oak, *Q. stellata* var. *paludosa* Sarg. (Mississippi Valley oak). Small to medium-sized (rarely large) tree of eastern half of United States except northern border. Bark reddish brown, fissured into broad, scaly ridges. Leaves oblong or obovate, 4–8 in (10–20 cm) long, usually wedge-shaped at base, deeply 5–7-lobed (3-lobed in a variety), the lobes broad and 2 middle lobes largest (with base and apex forming a cross), dark green and rough above, grayish hairy beneath, turning brown in fall. Acorns ½–1 in (12–25 mm) long, nearly half enclosed by deep cup.
Principal uses: Railroad crossties and construction timbers.

120. White oak, *Quercus alba* L. (stave oak). Large tree of eastern half of United States and adjacent Canada. Bark light gray, fissured into scaly ridges. Leaves elliptic, 4–9 in (10–23 cm) long, deeply or shallowly 5–9-lobed, hairless, bright green above, pale or whitish beneath, turning deep red in fall. Acorns ¾–1 in (20–25 mm) long, with shallow cup.
Principal uses: The most important lumber tree of the white oak group and one of the best oaks with high-grade all-purpose wood. The outstanding wood for tight barrels. Shade tree. (State tree of Connecticut and Maryland.)

WESTERN

Tree species Nos. 121–180 are native within the western half of continental United States, west of the prairie-plains and including Alaska. Also, the following 12 species of eastern trees are partly western: Nos. 16, 33, 37, 80, 81, 83, 88, 92, 93, 96, 113, 117. These 5 species of eastern trees range also beyond to Alaska: Nos. 2, 16, 17, 83, 88.

GYMNOSPERMS (CONIFERS OR SOFTWOODS)

A (*AA* on p. 48). Trees resinous, with leaves needlelike or scalelike, evergreen (except larch, No. 121); seeds borne on scales of a cone (berrylike in juniper, Nos. 154–157, or seeds single in a fleshy scarlet cup in yew, No. 134)—**Gymnosperms** (conifers or softwoods, such as pines, spruces, firs).

B. Leaves shedding in fall, needlelike, many in cluster on short, spur branches—**Larch** (*Larix*; see also No. 2).

121. Western larch, *Larix occidentalis* Nutt. (hackmatack, Montana larch, mountain larch, tamarack, western tamarack). Large tree of mountains of Northwestern United States and Southeastern British Columbia. Bark reddish brown, scaly, becoming deeply furrowed into flat ridges with many overlapping plates. Needles many in cluster on short, spur branches (or single on leading twigs), 3-angled, 1–1¼ in (2.5–3 cm) long, light pale green, shedding in fall. Cones upright 1–1½ in (2.5–4 cm) long, with long, pointed bracts.
Principal uses: Lumber for construction, interior paneling, flooring, crates, pallets, and railway-cars. Utility poles, piling, and mine-shaft guides. Plywood. Pulpwood. Chemical products, such as medicines and baking powder, can be made from the natural sugar (galactan) in gum and wood. Ornamental.

BB. Leaves evergreen, needlelike or scalelike, single or not more than 5 in a cluster.
C. Leaves in clusters of 2–5 (1 in No. 133), with sheath at base, needlelike—**Pine** (*Pinus*).
D. Needles 5 in a cluster—**White (soft) pines.**

122. Bristlecone pine, *Pinus aristata* Engelm. (foxtail pine, Intermountain bristlecone pine, Colorado bristlecone pine, hickory pine; *P. longaeva* D. K. Bailey). Small to medium-sized tree of high altitudes in Rocky Mountains and Great Basin. (The world's oldest known

121. **Western larch.** 122. **Bristlecone pine.** 123. **Limber pine.** 124. **Western white pine.**

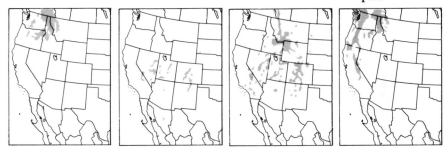

living dated trees, a few more than 4,600 years old.) Bark smoothish gray, becoming irregularly fissured, scaly, and reddish brown. Needles numerous and densely crowded, 5 in a cluster, 1–1½ in (2.5–4 cm) long, stout, dark green, curved and pressed against twig, persistent many years in "foxtails." Cones 2½–4 in (6–10 cm) long, dark purplish brown, scales with slender prickles.

Principal use: Mine timbers.

123. Limber pine, *Pinus flexilis* James (Rocky Mountain white pine, white pine). Medium-sized tree of Rocky Mountain region, including adjacent Canada. Bark dark brown, furrowed into rectangular, scaly plates. Needles 5 in cluster, slender, 2–3½ in (5–9 cm) long, dark green. Cones short-stalked, 3–6 in (7.5–15 cm) long, yellow brown, with thick, rounded scales and large seeds ⅜–½ in (10–12 mm) long.

Principal uses: Lumber (mostly for rough construction and occasionally for boxes), railroad crossties, poles, and fuel.

124. Western white pine, *Pinus monticola* Dougl. (mountain white pine, Idaho white pine, white pine). Large tree of northern Rocky Mountain and Pacific coast regions, including southern British Columbia. Bark gray, thin, smoothish, becoming fissured into rectangular, scaly plates. Needles 5 in cluster, stout, 2–4 in (5–10 cm) long, blue green. Cones long-stalked, 5–12 in (13–30 cm) long, yellow brown, dark red, or purple, with thin, rounded scales.

Principal uses: Important timber tree. Lumber for building construction, interior paneling, windows, panel doors, trim, moldings, patterns, furniture. Plywood. Pulpwood. A leading match wood. (State tree of Idaho.)

125. Sugar pine, *Pinus lambertiana* Dougl. (California sugar pine). Very large tree (world's largest pine) of Pacific coast region from Oregon to Baja California. Bark brown, furrowed into irregular, scaly ridges. Needles 5 in cluster, stout, 3–4 in (7.5–10 cm) long, blue green. Cones long-stalked, very large, 12–18 in (30–45 cm) long. yellow brown, with thin, rounded scales.

Principal uses: Lumber for building construction, boxes and crates, millwork, and foundry patterns.

    DD. Needles 3 or fewer in a cluster—**Yellow (hard) pines** (Nos. 126–131) and **pinyons** (or nut pines, Nos. 132 and 133).
      E. Needles more than 4 in (10 cm) long.

39

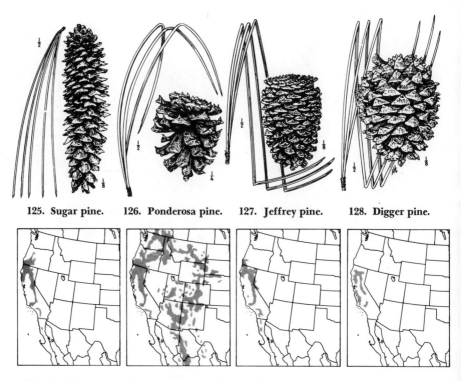

125. Sugar pine.   126. Ponderosa pine.   127. Jeffrey pine.   128. Digger pine.

126. Ponderosa pine, *Pinus ponderosa* Dougl. ex Laws. (Rocky Mountain ponderosa pine, western yellow pine, yellow pine, ponderosa pine, Arizona pine, blackjack pine, bull pine, rock pine, pino real). Large tree of Rocky Mountain and Pacific coast regions, including adjacent Canada and Mexico (the most widely distributed pine in North America). Bark brown or blackish, furrowed into ridges; on older trunks becoming yellow brown and irregularly fissured into large, flat, scaly plates. Needles 3 or 2 and 3 in cluster, stout, 4–7 in (10–18 cm) long, dark green. Cones short-stalked, 3–6 in (7.5–15 cm) long, light reddish brown, the scales with prickles.

Principal uses: Important timber tree, the most important western pine, and second to Douglas-fir in total stand in the United States. Lumber for many uses, such as building construction, boxes, furniture. The major species for windows and panel doors. Patterns, toys, caskets, and luggage. Posts, poles, and pulpwood. Christmas trees and decorations. Shelterbelts, ornamental, and shade tree. (State tree of Montana.)

127. Jeffrey pine, *Pinus jeffreyi* Grev. & Balf. (western yellow pine, bull pine, black pine, ponderosa pine). Large tree of Pacific coast region from Oregon to Lower California. Bark purplish brown, becoming fissured into large plates. Needles 3 in cluster, stout, 5–10 in (13–25 cm) long, blue green. Cones short-stalked, 5–10 in (13–25 cm) long, light brown, scales with prickles.

Principal uses: Lumber sold as ponderosa pine (No. 126) and has similar uses.

128. Digger pine, *Pinus sabiniana* Dougl. (gray pine, bull pine). Medium-sized tree of California foothills. Bark dark brown, furrowed into broad, irregular, scaly ridges. Needles 3 in cluster, slender and drooping, 8–12 in (20–30 cm) long, pale blue green. Cones long-stalked, 6–10 in (15–25 cm) long, red brown, with stout scales ending in curved spines. Seeds ¾–⅞ in (20–22 mm) long, edible.

Principal uses: Fuel. Shelterbelts. Edible seeds.

129. Knobcone pine, *Pinus attenuata* Lemm. Small to medium-sized tree of southwestern Oregon and California. Bark brown, thin, fissured into large, scaly ridges. Needles 3 in cluster, slender, 3–7 in (7.5–18 cm) long, yellowish green. Cones usually clustered and abundant, 1-sided, 3–6 in (7.5–15 cm) long, light yellow brown, with prickly scales, remaining closed on tree indefinitely.

Principal uses: Fuel. Shelterbelts.

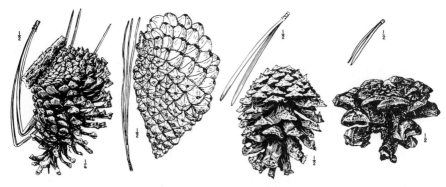

129. Knobcone pine.   130. Monterey pine.   131. Lodgepole   132. Pinyon.
                                              pine.

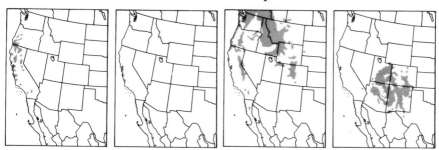

130. Monterey pine, *Pinus radiata* D. Don. Medium-sized to large tree rare and very local on coast of central California including Santa Cruz and Santa Rosa Islands and Guadalupe Island of Mexico. Bark dark reddish brown, deeply furrowed into scaly plates. Needles 3 in cluster, slender, 4–6 in (10–15 cm) long, green. Cones egg-shaped, pointed at apex, very 1-sided at base, short-stalked, turned back, 3–5½ in (7.5–14 cm) long, shiny brown, prickly, the scales on outer side near base much thickened, remaining closed on tree.

Principal uses: The most common pine in forest plantations in the southern hemisphere for pulpwood and lumber. Shade and ornament.

    EE. Needles less than 3 in (7.5 cm) long.

131. Lodgepole pine, *Pinus contorta* Dougl. (black pine, scrub pine, tamarack pine). Varieties: shore pine, var. *contorta*, of Pacific coast; lodgepole pine (Rocky Mountain), var. *latifolia* Engelm; Sierra lodgepole pine, var. *murrayana* (Grev. & Balf.) Engelm. Medium-sized to large tree of Rocky Mountain and Pacific coast regions including southeast Alaska, adjacent Canada, and Baja California. Bark gray or brown, thin, with many loose scales. Needles 2 in cluster, stout, often twisted, 1–3 in (2.5–7.5 cm) long, yellow green. Cones egg-shaped, 1-sided, ¾–2 in (2–5 cm) long, light yellow brown or dark green with prickly scales usually remaining closed on tree many years.

Principal uses: Lumber, including knotty pine paneling, cabinetwork, and interior finish. Mine timbers, fence posts, poles, utility poles. Pulpwood.

132. Pinyon, *Pinus edulis* Engelm. (two-leaf pinyon, two-needle pinyon, Colorado pinyon, nut pine, "pinyon pine," piñón; *Pinus cembroides* var. *edulis* (Engelm.) Voss). Small tree of southern Rocky Mountain region, mainly in foothills. Bark reddish brown, furrowed into scaly ridges. Needles 2 (sometimes 3) in cluster, stout, ¾–1½ in (2–4 cm) long, dark green. Cones egg-shaped, 1½–2 in (4–5 cm) long, light brown, with stout, blunt scales and large wingless, edible seeds ½ in (12 mm) long.

Principal uses: The edible seeds are a wild, commercial nut crop, sold as pinyon nuts and Indian nuts. Mine timbers and fuel. Ornamental. Christmas trees. (State tree of New Mexico.)

133. Singleleaf pinyon, *Pinus monophylla* Torr. & Frém. (pinyon, nut pine, "singleleaf pinyon pine," piñón; *Pinus cembroides* var. *monophylla* (Torr. & Frém.) Voss). Small tree

41

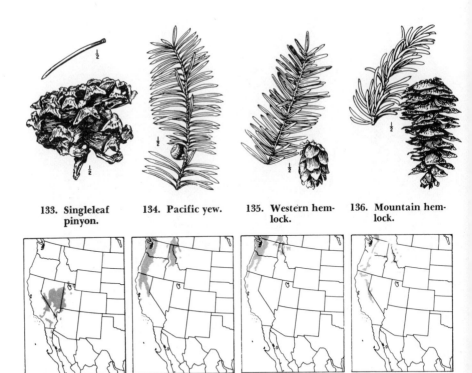

| 133. Singleleaf pinyon. | 134. Pacific yew. | 135. Western hemlock. | 136. Mountain hemlock. |

of Great Basin region to California and Baja California. Bark dark brown, furrowed into scaly ridges. Needles 1 in a sheath, stout, 1–2 in (2.5–5 cm) long, gray green. Cones egg-shaped, 2–2½ in (5–6 cm) long, light brown, with stout, blunt scales, and large wingless, thin-shelled edible seeds ¾ in (20 mm) long.

Principal uses: The edible seeds are sold locally as pinyon nuts and pine nuts. Mine timbers and fuel. (State tree of Nevada.)

    CC. Leaves borne singly and not in clusters, without sheath at base, needlelike or scalelike.
        F. (FF on page 46), Leaves needlelike, mostly more than ½ in (12 mm) long.
            G. Twigs roughened by projecting bases of old needles.
                H. Needles with leafstalk, flattened, appearing in 2 rows (half-round and extending in No. 136).
                    I. Needles stiff, sharp-pointed, extending down twig—**Yew** (*Taxus*).

134. Pacific yew, *Taxus brevifolia* Nutt. (western yew). Small to medium-sized tree of Pacific Coast and northern Rocky Mountain regions north to Canada and southeast Alaska. Bark purplish brown, very thin, smoothish, with papery scales. Needles in 2 rows, flat, slightly curved, paler beneath, stiff, sharp-pointed, ½–1 in (12–25 cm) long, dark yellow green, leafstalks extending down twigs. Seeds single, ⅜ in (10 mm) long (poisonous), exposed at apex but partly surrounded by a thick, fleshy, scarlet cup.

Principal uses: Poles, canoe paddles, bows, and small cabinetwork. Ornamental.

                    II. Needles soft, blunt-pointed, not extending down twig—**Hemlock** (*Tsuga*).

135. Western hemlock, *Tsuga heterophylla* (Raf.) Sarg. (Pacific hemlock, west coast hemlock). Large tree of Pacific coast and northern Rocky Mountain regions north to Canada and Alaska. Bark purplish brown, deeply furrowed into bread, flat ridges. Needles short-stalked, flat, ¼–¾ in (6–20 mm) long, shiny dark green, lighter beneath. Cones ¾–1 in (2–2.5 cm) long, brownish.

Principal uses: Important timber tree. Pulpwood (one of the best). Construction, interior finish, boxes and crates, flooring, and veneer for plywood. Railroad crossties, mine timbers, and marine piling. The bark is a potential source of tannin. Ornamental. (State tree of Washington.)

137. Engelmann spruce. 138. Blue spruce. 139. Sitka spruce. 140. Douglas-fir.

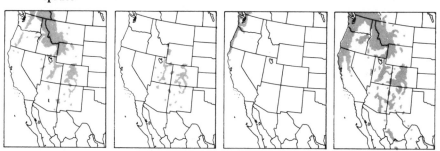

136. Mountain hemlock, *Tsuga mertensiana* (Bong.) Carr. (black hemlock, alpine hemlock). Large to small tree of mountains to timber line, Pacific coast and northern Rocky Mountain regions north to Canada and Alaska. Bark reddish brown, deeply furrowed into narrow ridges. Needles short-stalked, half-round or angled, ¼–1 in (6–25 mm) long, blue green. Cones 1–2½ in (2.5–6 cm) long, usually purplish or green, turning brown.
    Principal uses: Same as No. 135.

> *HH.* Needles without leafstalk, 4-angled (flat in No. 139), sharp-pointed, extending out on all sides of twig—**Spruce** (*Picea*; see also Nos. 16 and 17).

137. Engelmann spruce, *Picea engelmannii* Parry (Columbian spruce, mountain spruce, silver spruce, white spruce). Large tree of high mountains, Rocky Mountain and Pacific coast regions, including adjacent Canada. Bark grayish or purplish brown, thin, with loosely attached scales. Needles 4-angled, ⅝–1⅛ in (15–28 mm) long, dark or pale blue green, of disagreeable odor when crushed. Cones 1½–2½ in (4–6 cm) long, light brown, with long, thin, flexible scales irregularly toothed and more or less pointed.
    Principal uses: Home construction, plywood. Piano sounding boards, violins, boxes, crates, prefabricated wood products, specialty items, furniture. Pulpwood. Ornamental.

138. Blue spruce, *Picea pungens* Engelm. (Colorado blue spruce, Colorado spruce, silver spruce). Large tree of Rocky Mountain region. Bark gray or brown, furrowed into scaly ridges. Needles 4-angled, ¾–1⅛ in (20–28 mm) long, dull blue green. Cones 2¼–4 in (6–10 cm) long, light brown, with long, thin, flexible scales irregularly toothed and more or less pointed.
    Principal uses: Ornamental and shelterbelts. Posts, poles, and fuel. (State tree of Colorado and Utah.)

139. Sitka spruce, *Picea sitchensis* (Bong.) Carr. (coast spruce, tideland spruce, yellow spruce). Large to very large tree (the largest native spruce) of Pacific coast region north to Canada and Alaska. Bark reddish brown, thin, with loosely attached scales. Needles flat, ⅝–1 in (15–25 mm) long, dark green. Cones 2–3½ in (5–9 cm) long, light orange brown, with long, stiff scales, rounded and irregularly toothed.
    Principal uses: Manufactured products, including piano sounding boards, siding, food containers, cooperage, venetian blinds, boat construction items, door cuttings, cabinets, scaffold planking, and aircraft items. Pulpwood. Formerly an important wood for aircraft construction. Ornamental. (State tree of Alaska.)

43

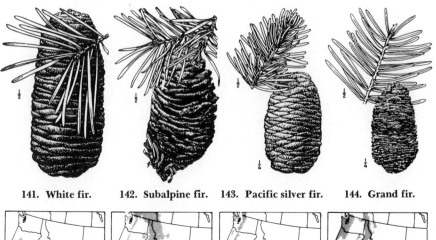

| 141. White fir. | 142. Subalpine fir. | 143. Pacific silver fir. | 144. Grand fir. |

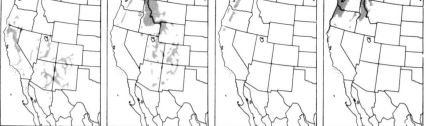

GG. Twigs smooth or nearly so.
  J. Needles with short leafstalks; cones hanging down, with 3-toothed bracts—
    Douglas-fir (*Pseudotsuga*).

140. Douglas-fir, *Pseudotsuga menziesii* (Mirb.) Franco (red-fir, Oregon-pine, Douglas-spruce, coast Douglas-fir, Oregon Douglas-fir, Rocky Mountain Douglas-fir, inland Douglas-fir, Colorado Douglas-fir; *Ps. douglasii* (Sabine) Carr., *Ps. mucronata* (Raf.) Sudw., *Ps. taxifolia* (Poir.) Britton). Very large tree (next to giant sequoia and redwood in size) of Pacific coast and Rocky Mountain regions, including Canada and Mexico. Bark reddish brown, thick, deeply furrowed into broad ridges. Needles short-stalked, flat, ¾–1¼ in (20–30 mm) long, dark yellow green or blue green. Cones 2–4 in (5–10 cm) long, light brown, with thin, rounded scales and long, 3-toothed bracts.
  Principal uses: Important timber tree, first in United States in total stand volume, lumber production, and production of veneer for plywood. Used mainly for building construction as lumber, timbers, piling, and plywood. Also railroad crossties, cooperage, mine timbers, and fencing. Lumber manufactured into millwork, railroad-car construction, boxes and crates, flooring, furniture, ships and boats, ladders. Pulpwood. Also shade tree, ornamental, and shelterbelts. (State tree of Oregon.)

    JJ. Needles without leafstalks; cones upright, in top of tree—**Fir** (*Abies*; see also
      No. 19).
      K. Needles flat.

141. White fir, *Abies concolor* (Gord. & Glend.) Lindl. (concolor fir, silver fir, white balsam, balsam fir). Variety: California white fir, var. *lowiana* (Gord.) Lemm. (Pacific white fir). Mountain and Pacific coast regions, south to northwestern Mexico. Bark gray, smoothish, becoming thick, deeply furrowed into scaly ridges. Needles flat, 1½–2½ in (4–6 cm) long, pale blue green. Cones upright, 3–5 in (7.5–13 cm) long, greenish, purple, or yellow.
  Principal uses: Lumber for construction, including framing, sheathing, flooring, interior trim and millwork, paneling, and sash and doors. Industrial uses such as boxes and crates, food containers, and plywood products. Pulpwood. Ornamental and shade tree.

142. Subalpine fir, *Abies lasiocarpa* (Hook.) Nutt. (alpine fir, balsam, white balsam, balsam fir, white fir). Medium-sized to large tree of high mountains, Rocky Mountain

44

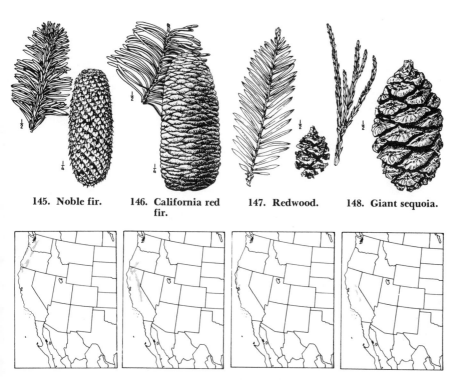

145. Noble fir.   **146. California red fir.**   **147. Redwood.**   **148. Giant sequoia.**

region north to Canada and southeast Alaska. Bark gray, smoothish, becoming fissured. Needles flat, 1–1¾ in (25–45 mm) long, blue green. Cones upright, 2¼–4 in (6–10 cm) long, purple.

Principal uses: Same as No. 141.

143. Pacific silver fir, *Abies amabilis* (Dougl.) Forbes. (lovely fir, silver fir, amabilis fir, red fir, Cascades fir). Large tree of Pacific coast region from Oregon north to western British Columbia and extreme southeast Alaska. Bark gray, smoothish, becoming rough and scaly. Needles flat or pointing forward, ¾–1¼ in (20–30 mm) long, dark green and shiny, silvery white beneath. Cones upright, 3–6 in (7.5–15 cm) long, purple.

Principal uses: Same as No. 141.

144. Grand fir, *Abies grandis* (Dougl.) Lindl. (lowland white fir, lowland fir, balsam fir, white fir, silver fir, yellow fir). Large tree of northern Rocky Mountain and Pacific coast regions, including southern British Columbia. Bark brown, becoming deeply furrowed into narrow ridges. Needles flat, in 2 rows 1–2 in (25–50 mm) long, dark green and shiny, silvery white beneath. Cones upright, 2–4 in (5–10 cm) long, green or brown.

Principal uses: Same as No. 141.

            KK. Needles 4-angled, or both 4-angled and flat.

145. Noble fir, *Abies procera* Rehd. (red fir, white fir; *A. nobilis* (Dougl.) Lindl., not A. Dietr.). Large tree (one of the largest true firs) of Northwest Pacific coast region. Bark gray brown and smoothish, becoming brown to red brown, furrowed and broken into irregular scaly plates. Needles of lower branches flat and of top branches 4-angled, 1–1½ in (25–38 mm) long, blue green. Cones upright, 4–6 in (10–15 cm) long, purplish brown, with long greenish or reddish bracts covering cone scales.

Principal uses: Same as No. 141.

146. California red fir, *Abies magnifica* A. Murr. (red fir, silvertip, golden fir, white fir, Shasta fir, Shasta red fir). Large tree (largest native true fir) of mountains in southwestern Oregon, California, and extreme western Nevada. Bark reddish brown, thick, deeply furrowed into narrow ridges. Needles 4-angled, ¾–1½ in (20–38 mm) long, blue green. Cones upright, 6–9 in (15–23 cm) long, purplish brown.

Principal uses: Same as No. 141.

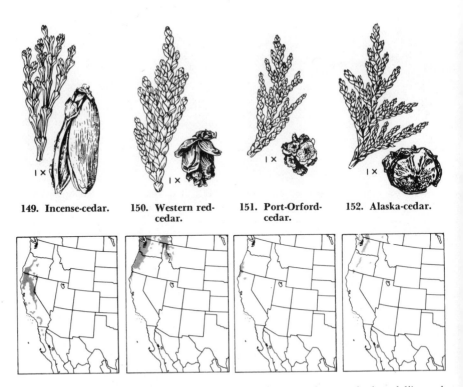

149. Incense-cedar. **150. Western red-cedar.** **151. Port-Orford-cedar.** **152. Alaska-cedar.**

FF (*F* on p. 42). Leaves scalelike, less than ¼ in (6 mm) long, or both scalelike and needlelike to ¾ in (20 mm) long.
  L. Leaves single.
    M. Leaves both scalelike and needlelike—**Redwood** (*Sequoia sempervirens*).

147. Redwood, *Sequoia sempervirens* (D. Don) Endl. (coast redwood, California redwood). Very large tree (world's tallest) of Pacific coast in California and extreme southwestern Oregon. Bark reddish brown, very thick, deeply furrowed, fibrous. Leaves both scalelike and needlelike, flat, slightly curved, unequal in length, ¼–¾ in (6–20 mm) long, dark green, spreading in 2 rows. Cones ¾–1 in (2–2.5 cm) long, reddish brown, maturing first year.

Principal uses: Important timber tree. Building construction, beams, bridges, and other heavy construction. Manufactured building products, such as siding, sash, doors, and veneer for plywood and box products; wooden furniture and fixtures; and refrigeration and cooling equipment. Specialty products and decorative wood products from burls. Insulating material is made from the bark. Ornamental and shade tree. (California redwood, including No. 148, is the State tree of California.)

  MM. Leaves scalelike—**Giant sequoia** (*Sequoiadendron giganteum*).

148. Giant sequoia, *Sequoiadendron giganteum* (Lindl.) Buchholz (sequoia, bigtree, Sierra redwood; *Sequoia wellingtonia* Seem., *Sequoia gigantea* (Lindl.) Decne., not Endl.). Very large tree (world's largest in volume, weight, and trunk diameter; among the oldest, after bristlecone pine, and tallest, after redwood), with swollen base, Sierra Nevada, California. Bark reddish brown, thick, deeply furrowed fibrous. Leaves scalelike, ⅛–¼ in (3–6 mm) long or on leading shoots ½ in (12 mm) long, blue green, sharp-pointed, growing all around twig and overlapping. Cones 1¾–2¾ in (4.5–7 cm) long, reddish brown, maturing second year.

Principal uses: Almost all trees are preserved in National Parks, National Forests, a State Park, and a State Forest. Formerly lumbered for the same uses as No. 147.

  LL. Leaves in pairs, 3's, or 4's, scalelike.
    N. Leafy twigs more or less flattened.
      O. Twigs much flattened, more than 1/16 in (1.5 mm) broad including leaves.
        P. Joints of leafy twigs distinctly longer than broad—**Incense-cedar** (*Libocedrus decurrens*).

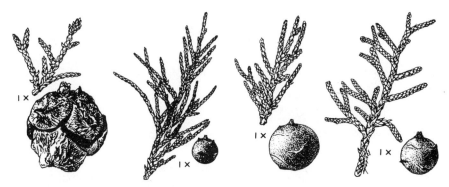

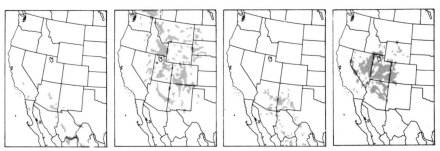

153. Arizona cypress.   154. Rocky Mountain   155. Alligator juni-   156. Utah juniper.
                             juniper.   per.

149. Incense-cedar, *Libocedrus decurrens* Torr. (*Calocedrus decurrens* (Torr.) Florin). Large tree of Pacific coast region from Oregon to Baja California. Bark reddish brown, thick, deeply and irregularly furrowed into shreddy ridges. Twigs flattened, joints wedge-shaped, $\frac{1}{8}$–$\frac{1}{2}$ in (3–12 mm) long, bright green, with scale leaves $\frac{1}{16}$–$\frac{1}{8}$ in (1.5–3 mm) long, their bases extending down twigs. Cones $\frac{3}{4}$–1 in. (2–2.5 cm) long, reddish brown.

Principal uses: Exterior siding, sheathing, subflooring, interior paneling, woodwork. Toys and novelties. Fence posts, rails, and poles. The leading wood for pencils. Ornamental and shade tree.

   PP. Joints of leafy twigs about as long as broad—**Thuja** (*Thuja*).

150. Western redcedar, *Thuja plicata* Donn ex D. Don (Pacific redcedar, giant-cedar, arborvitae, giant arborvitae, canoe-cedar, shinglewood). Large to very large tree (second in maximum trunk diameter) of Pacific coast and northern Rocky Mountain regions north to Canada and southeast Alaska. Bark reddish brown, thin, fibrous. Twigs flattened and branching in one plane. Leaves scalelike, $\frac{1}{16}$–$\frac{1}{8}$ in (1.5–3 mm) long, shiny, dark green. Cones $\frac{1}{2}$ in (12 mm) long, pale brown, with several paired leathery scales.

Principal uses: The chief wood for shingles. One of the most important lumber species for siding. Interior wall paneling, roof decking, caskets, wooden pipe and tanks, outdoor-patio construction, boatbuilding. A leading species for utility poles, fenceposts, and rails. Ornamental.

   OO. Twigs slightly flattened, less than $\frac{1}{16}$ in (1.5 mm) broad including leaves
   —**White-cedar** (*Chamaecyparis*).

151. Port-Orford-cedar, *Chamaecyparis lawsoniana* (A. Murr.) Parl. (Port-Orford white-cedar, Oregon-cedar, Lawson cypress). Large to very large tree of Pacific coast in south-western Oregon and northwestern California. Bark reddish brown, very thick, deeply fur-rowed into large, fibrous ridges. Twigs slender, flattened. Leaves $\frac{1}{16}$ in (1.5 mm) long, or $\frac{1}{8}$–$\frac{1}{4}$ in (3–6 mm) long on leading shoots, bright green or pale beneath, with gland dot on back. Cones about $\frac{3}{8}$ in (10 mm) in diameter.

Principal uses: Arrow shafts. Logs are exported to Japan for woodenware, novelties, and toys and construction in shrines and temples. Shade tree, ornamental, and shelterbelts.

152. Alaska-cedar, *Chamaecyparis nootkatensis* (D. Don) Spach (Alaska yellow-cedar, yellow-cedar, Nootka cypress, Sitka cypress, yellow cypress). Large tree of Northwest Pacific coast region north to Canada and Alaska. Bark grayish brown, thin, irregularly fissured, fibrous, and scaly. Twigs stout, 4-angled or slightly flattened. Leaves $\frac{1}{8}$ in (3 mm) long, or $\frac{1}{4}$ in (6 mm) long on leading shoots, dark green, usually without gland dot on back. Cones nearly $\frac{1}{2}$ in (12 mm) in diameter.

Principal uses: Construction, including flooring, bridges, culverts. Furniture, cabinet-work, interior finish, outdoor furniture, greenhouses. Utility poles, marine piling. Boats and canoes. Ornamental.

> NN. Leafy twigs rounded or 4-angled.
>> Q. Leafy twigs regularly branched almost at right angles; many seeds in a hard cone—**Cypress** (*Cupressus*).

153. Arizona cypress, *Cupressus arizonica* Greene (Arizona rough cypress, Arizona smooth cypress; *C. glabra* Sudw.). Medium-sized tree of Southwestern United States and adjacent Mexico. Bark gray, rough, furrowed and fibrous, or checkered, or smoothish and shedding in thin scales. Leaves scalelike, $\frac{1}{16}$ in (1.5 mm) long, pale blue green. Cones $\frac{3}{4}$–$1\frac{1}{4}$ in (2–3 cm) in diameter, on stout stalks $\frac{1}{4}$–$\frac{1}{2}$ in (6–12 mm) long, remaining attached several years.

Principal uses: Fenceposts, ornamental, and shelterbelts. Christmas trees.

>> QQ. Leafy twigs irregularly branched at small angles; seeds few in a soft "berry"—**Juniper** (*Juniperus*).

154. Rocky Mountain juniper, *Juniperus scopulorum* Sarg. (Rocky Mountain redcedar, redcedar, river juniper). Small to medium-sized tree of Rocky Mountain region, including adjacent Canada. Bark reddish brown, thin, fibrous and shreddy. Leafy twigs slender, about $\frac{1}{32}$ in (1 mm) in diameter. Leaves scalelike, $\frac{1}{16}$ in (1.5 mm) long, usually gray green, or on leading shoots needlelike, up to $\frac{1}{4}$ in (6 mm) long. "Berry" $\frac{1}{4}$ in (6 mm) in diameter, bright blue, bloomy, usually 2-seeded, maturing second year.

Principal uses: Fenceposts, fuel, lumber. Shelterbelts and ornamental.

155. Alligator juniper, *Juniperus deppeana* Steud. (checker-bark juniper; *J. pachyphloea* Torr.). Medium-sized tree of Southwestern United States and Mexico. Bark gray, thick, deeply furrowed into checkered or square plates. Leafy twigs $\frac{1}{32}$–$\frac{1}{16}$ in (1–1.5 mm) in diameter. Leaves scalelike, $\frac{1}{16}$ in (1.5 mm) long, blue green, with gland dot and often whitish resin drop on back, or on leading shoots needlelike, up to $\frac{1}{4}$ in (6 mm) long, pale or whitish. "Berry" $\frac{1}{2}$ in (12 mm) in diameter, bluish or brownish, bloomy, 4-seeded, maturing second year.

Principal uses: Fuel and fenceposts.

156. Utah juniper, *Juniperus osteosperma* (Torr.) Little (bigberry juniper; *J. utahensis* (Engelm.) Lemm.). Small tree of Great Basin and Rocky Mountain regions. Bark gray, fibrous, and shreddy. Leafy twigs stout, about $\frac{1}{16}$ in (1.5 mm) or less in diameter. Leaves $\frac{1}{16}$ in (1.5 mm) or more in length, yellow green. "Berry" $\frac{1}{4}$–$\frac{1}{2}$ in (6–12 mm) in diameter, brownish, bloomy, with 1 or 2 seeds.

Principal uses: Fenceposts, fuel, and interior finish.

157. Western juniper, *Juniperus occidentalis* Hook. (Sierra juniper). Small to medium-sized tree of Pacific coast region. Bark reddish brown, furrowed, and shreddy. Leafy twigs stout, $\frac{1}{16}$ in (1.5 mm) or more in diameter. Leaves scalelike, $\frac{1}{16}$ in (1.5 mm) or more in length, with gland dot on back. "Berry" $\frac{1}{4}$ in (6 mm) in diameter, bluish black, with 2 or 3 seeds.

Principal uses: Fenceposts, fuel, pencils.

ANGIOSPERMS (FLOWERING PLANTS)

AA (*A* on p. 38). Trees nonresinous, with leaves broad, shedding in fall in most species (evergreen in some oaks, tanoak, giant chinkapin, California-laurel, palms, etc.); seeds enclosed in a fruit—**Angiosperms** (flowering plants).

MONOCOTYLEDONS

> R. Leaves parallel-veined, evergreen, clustered at top of trunk or large branches; trunk with woody portions irregularly distributed, without clear distinction of bark and wood, and wihout annual rings—**Monocotyledons** (palms, yuccas, etc.).

158. Joshua-tree, *Yucca brevifolia* Engelm. Picturesque or grotesque small tree of Mohave desert (mostly in California and Nevada) with short stout trunk and broad open crown of many stout widely spreading branches. Trunks covered with dead leaves, becoming corky, rough, deeply furrowed into brown or gray plates. Leaves evergreen, many, long and narrow, mostly 8–14 in (20–36 cm) long, $\frac{1}{4}$–$\frac{1}{2}$ in (6–12 mm) wide, stiff, flattened, smooth or slightly rough, blue green, ending in short, sharp spine, the yellow edges bearing many

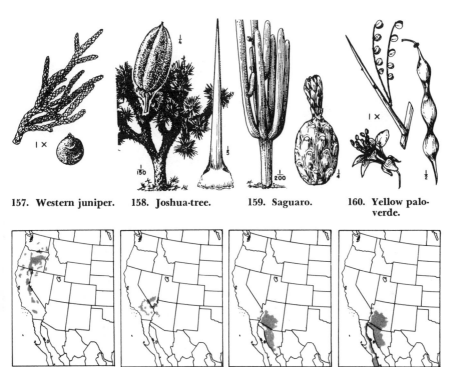

157. Western juniper.   **158. Joshua-tree.**   **159. Saguaro.**   **160. Yellow palo-verde.**

minute sharp teeth. Flowers many in terminal branched clusters, 1½–2½ in (4–6 cm) long, greenish yellow. Fruit egg-shaped, 2½–4 in (6–10 cm) long and 2 in (5 cm) in diameter, green to brown, fleshy.

Principal use: Ornamental.

DICOTYLEDONS (BROADLEAF TREES OR HARDWOODS)

RR. Leaves net-veined (rarely none); trunk with bark and wood distinct and with annual rings in wood—**Dicotyledons** (broadleaf trees, or hardwoods, such as oaks, poplars, ashes, maples).

   S. Leaves none (or soon shedding in No. 160); branches green, spiny.
      T. Trunk and the few branches cylindric, swollen, fleshy, with ridges bearing many spines in clusters—**Cereus** (*Cereus*).

159. Saguaro, *Cereus giganteus* Engelm. (giant cactus; *Carnegiea gigantea* (Engelm.) Britton & Rose). Giant columnar tree cactus or small spiny leafless tree of Arizona desert. Trunk and the few nearly erect branches cylindric, yellow green, with vertical fleshy ridges (or ribs) bearing clusters of spreading gray spines. Flowers many, funnel-shaped, 4–4½ in (10–11 cm) long, with many white petals. Fruits egg-shaped, 2–3½ in (5–9 cm) long, red, fleshy, sweet and edible, splitting open.

Principal use: Ornamental. (State flower of Arizona.)

      TT. Trunk and branches hard, woody, smooth, with green twigs ending in spines—**Paloverde** (*Cercidium*).

160. Yellow paloverde, *Cercidium microphyllum* (Torr.) Rose & Johnst. (foothill paloverde, littleleaf paloverde, small-leaf paloverde). Spiny small tree of Arizona desert and adjacent Mexico, with widely spreading, much-branched open crown, leafless most of year. Bark, branches, and twigs (some ending in spines) smooth, thin, yellow green. Leaves few, twice compound, ¾–1 in (2–2.5 cm) long, with short axis, 1 pair of branches, each with 4–7 pairs of very small yellow green elliptic leaflets less than ⅛ in (3 mm) long, soon shedding. Flowers numerous covering tree, beanlike, pale yellow, about ½ in (12 mm) long. Pods 2–3 in (5–7.5 cvm) long, ¼ in (6 mm) in diameter, cylindric, 1–3-seeded, narrowed between seeds.

Principal use: Ornamental. (Paloverde, *Cercidium* spp., is the State tree of Arizona.)

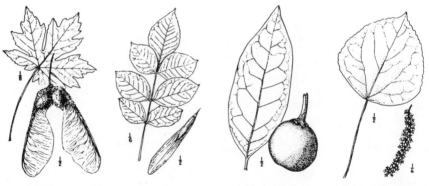

161. Bigleaf maple.   **162. Oregon ash.**   **163. California-laurel.**   **164. Quaking aspen.**

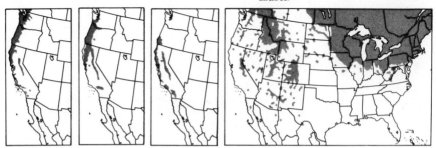

SS. Leaves produced; branches usually gray or brown, not spiny.
    U. Leaves and usually branc¹ es in pairs (opposite).
        V. Leaves not divided into leaflets (simple), deeply 3–5-lobed—**Maple** (*Acer*).

161. Bigleaf maple, *Acer macrophyllum* Pursh (broadleaf maple, Oregon maple). Large tree of Pacific coast region from southern California north to British Columbia. Bark gray brown, thin, smoothish, becoming deeply furrowed. Leaves paired, very large, as broad as long, 6–12 in (15–30 cm) in diameter, deeply 3- or 5-lobed with additional smaller lobes, dark green and shiny above, pale green below, turning bright yellow to tan in fall. Leaf-stalks long and stout, 10–12 in (25–30 cm) long. Key fruits 1¼–2 in (3–5 cm) long, long-winged, paired, and in clusters.
Principal uses: Veneer, furniture, handles and fixtures, and woodenware and novelties. Shade tree.

        VV. Leaves divided into 5–9 leaflets (compound)—**Ash** (*Fraxinus;* see also Nos. 33 and 37).

162. Oregon ash, *Fraxinus latifolia* Benth. (*F. oregona* Nutt.). Medium-sized to large tree of Pacific coast region from Washington to California. Bark dark gray or brown, with diamond-shaped fissures and forking ridges. Leaves paired, compound, 5–14 in (13–36 cm) long. Leaflets usually 7 or 5, usually without stalks, elliptic, 2–5 in (5–13 cm) long, short-pointed, edges often slightly toothed, light green nearly hairless above, finely hairy beneath. Key fruits in crowded custers, 1–2 in (2.5–5 cm) long, with wing at end.
Principal uses: Same as No. 36. Shade tree.

    UU. Leaves and usually branches borne singly (alternate).
        W. Leaves aromatic when bruised—**California-laurel** (*Umbellularia californica*).

163. California-laurel, *Umbellularia californica* (Hook. & Arn.) Nutt. (Oregon-myrtle, California-bay, Pacific-myrtle, pepperwood, spice-tree). Medium-sized to large tree of Oregon and California. Bark dark reddish brown, thin, with flat scales. Leaves aromatic, evergreen, elliptic or lance-shaped, 2–5 in (5–13 cm) long, short-stalked, wedge-shaped at base, short-pointed, not toothed on edges, leathery, hairless, shiny dark green above, dull beneath. Flowers yellowish green, ³⁄₁₆ in (5 mm) long, in clusters. Fruits rounded, 1 in (2.5 cm) in diameter, greenish or purplish.
Principal uses: Veneer for furniture and paneling. Novelties and woodenware, cabinet-work and interior trim. Ornamental.

50

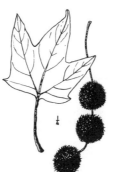

| 165. Black cotton-wood. | 166. California syca-more. | 167. Netleaf hack-berry. | 168. Red alder. |

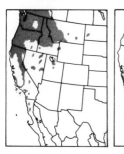

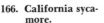

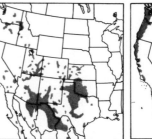

WW. Leaves not aromatic.
  X. Winter buds 1 or none at tip of twig; fruit not an acorn.
    Y. Leaves thin, with edges toothed, shedding in fall.
      Z. Leafstalks more than 1½ in (4 cm) long, slender, leaves almost as broad as long; seeds cottony or hairy.
        a. Leaves with 1 main vein, toothed but not lobed—**Cottonwood, poplar** (*Populus*; see also Nos. 81 and 83).

164. Quaking aspen, *Populus tremuloides* Michx. (trembling aspen, aspen, golden aspen, mountain aspen, trembling poplar, poplar, popple). Small to medium-sized tree, widely distributed in Northeastern, Rocky Mountain, and Pacific coast regions and across Canada to Alaska. (The most widespread hardwood in North America.) Bark yellowish green or whitish, smooth, thin; on large trunks becoming black, thick, with furrows and flat ridges. Leaves nearly round, 1¼–3 in (4–7.5 cm) long, short-pointed, finely toothed, hairless, shiny green above, dull green beneath. Leafstalks flat. Seeds rarely produced in the West.
Principal uses: Pulpwood for paper and insulation board. Boxes, crating pallets, furniture parts, lumber core and interior trim, panel stock, match and cone stock, excelsior, particle-board, paper roll plugs, and turned products.

165. Black cottonwood, *Populus trichocarpa* Torr. & Gray (California poplar, balsam cottonwood, western balsam poplar). Large tree (the tallest western broadleaf tree) of northern Rocky Mountain and Pacific coast regions north to Canada and Alaska. Bark gray, smooth at first, becoming deeply furrowed with flat ridges. Leaves broadly oval, 3–7 in (7.5–18 cm) long, short- or long-pointed, finely toothed, often slightly hairy, dark shiny green above, whitish or rusty beneath. Leafstalks round.
Principal uses: Boxes and crates, pulpwood, and excelsior.

        aa. Leaves with 5 or 3 main veins from base and 5 or 3 lobes—**Sycamore** (*Platanus*).

166. California sycamore, *Platanus racemosa* Nutt. (California planetree, western syca-more, aliso). Large tree with broad trunk, of wet soils in California and adjacent Mexico. Bark of branches whitish, thin, smooth; bark of trunk smoothish and peeling off in brownish flakes, becoming thick, dark gray, and deeply furrowed. Leaves 5–8 in (13–20 cm) long and broad, with 5 or 3 main veins from base, deeply divided into 5 or 3 narrow lobes, toothed, light green above, paler and hairy beneath. Many minute hairy fruits in 2–7 balls

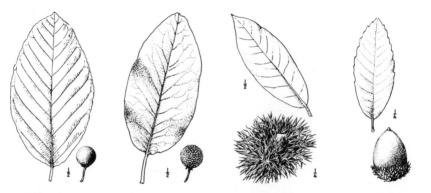

169. Cascara buck- **170. Pacific madrone.** **171. Giant chinka-** **172. Tanoak.**
    thorn.   **pin.**

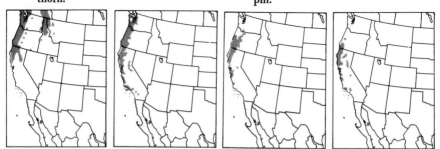

⅞ in (2.2 cm) in diameter along a stalk.
   Principal uses: Shade. Ornament.

        ZZ. Leafstalks less than 1 in (2.5 cm) long, leaves elliptic or oval; seeds not
           hairy.
           b. Leaves with 3 main veins from base and with the 2 sides unequal—
              Hackberry (*Celtis;* see also No. 79).

   167. Netleaf hackberry, *Celtis reticulata* Torr. (western hackberry, palo blanco; *C. douglasii* Planch.) Small tree of western half of United States and Northern Mexico. Bark gray,
smoothish or becoming rough, with corky warts. Leaves in 2 rows, mostly ovate, 1–2½ in
(2.5–6 cm) long, the 2 sides unequal, edges sometimes saw-toothed, with 3 main veins from
base, usually thick, dark green and rough above, paler and slightly hairy beneath. Fruits
¼–⅜ in (6–10 mm) in diameter, orange red, 1-seeded.
   Principal use: Fenceposts.

        bb. Leaves with 1 main vein and with both sides equal.
           c. Leaf edges with teeth of 2 sizes and slightly irregular—**Alder** (*Alnus;*
             see also No. 88).

   168. Red alder, *Alnus rubra* Bong. (Oregon alder, western alder, Pacific coast alder).
Medium-sized to large tree of Pacific coast region north to British Columbia and southeast
Alaska. Bark mottled light gray to whitish, smooth, thin. Leaves oval or elliptic, 3–6 in
(7.5–15 cm) long, short-pointed, both coarsely and finely toothed, dark green and
nearly hairless above, grayish green or rusty hairy beneath. Cones ½–1 in (12–25 mm) long.
   Principal uses: The leading hardwood in the Pacific Northwest. Pulpwood. Furniture,
cabinetwork, fixtures, general millwork, and handles.

           cc. Leaf edges with uniform, small teeth—**Buckthorn** (*Rhamnus;* see
             also No. 93).

   169. Cascara buckthorn, *Rhamnus purshiana* DC. (cascara sagrada, cascara). Small tree
or shrub of northwest Pacific coast and northern Rocky Mountain regions north to British
Columbia. Bark brown or gray, thin, scaly. Leaves elliptic, 2–6 in (5–15 cm) long, blunt-
pointed or rounded, finely toothed, dark green above, lighter and slightly hairy beneath.
Fruits berrylike, ⅜–½ in (10–12 mm) in diameter, purplish black, with 2 or 3 seeds.
   Principal uses: The bark is the source of the drug Cascara Sagrada. Fenceposts.
Ornamental.

| 173. California black oak. | 174. Coast live oak. | 175. Emory oak. | 176. Canyon live oak. |

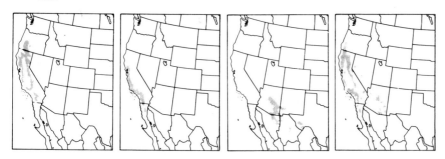

YY. Leaves thick, without teeth (sometimes toothed in No. 170), evergreen.
    d. Leaves pale or whitish beneath—**Madrone** (*Arbutus*).

170. Pacific madrone, *Arbutus menziesii* Pursh (madrone, madrona, madroño). Small to large tree of Pacific coast region north to British Columbia. Bark of limbs and twigs bright red, smooth and peeling off; bark of larger trunks dark reddish brown, fissured and scaly. Leaves evergreen, oval, 3–5 in (7.5–13 cm) long, blunt-pointed, thick and leathery, edges sometimes toothed, dark green and shiny above, whitish beneath. Flowers small, white, clustered ⅜ in (10 mm) long. Fruits ½ in (12 mm) in diameter, orange red.
Principal uses: Shuttles (used in textile weaving). Fuel. Ornamental.

        dd. Leaves with coat of golden yellow scales beneath—**Chinkapin** (*Castanopsis*).

171. Giant chinkapin, *Castanopsis chrysophylla* (Dougl.) A. DC. (golden chinkapin, giant evergreen-chinkapin, goldenleaf chestnut; *Chrysolepis chrysophylla* (Hook.) Hjelmqvist). Medium-sized to large tree (a variety is shrubby) of Pacific coast region. Bark reddish brown, becoming furrowed into thick plates. Leaves evergreen, oblong to lance-shaped, 2–6 in (5–15 cm) long, narrowed and tapering at both ends, without teeth on edges, leathery, dark green and shiny above, coated beneath with golden yellow scales. Fruits golden spiny burs 1–1½ in (2.5–4 cm) in diameter with 1 or sometimes 2 edible nuts ⅝ in (15 mm) long, maturing second year.
Principal uses: Furniture. Ornamental.

    XX. Winter buds 3 or more in cluster at tip of twig; fruit an acorn.
        e. Leaves with many parallel side veins less than ¼ in (6 mm) apart, evergreen; scales of acorn cup slender, spreading, curved, more than ⅛ in (3 mm) long—**Tanoak** (*Lithocarpus densiflorus*).

172. Tanoak, *Lithocarpus densiflorus* (Hook. & Arn.) Rehd. (tanbark-oak). Large tree (a variety is shrubby) of Oregon and California. Bark reddish brown, deeply fissured into squarish plates. Leaves evergreen, oblong, 3–5 in (7.5–13 cm) long, short-pointed, toothed, with many parallel side veins less than ¼ in (6 mm) apart, leathery, pale green, shiny and nearly hairless above, rusty-hairy or whitish beneath. Acorns ¾–1¼ in (20–30 mm) long, rounded, the shallow cup with spreading light brown scales ⅛–³⁄₁₆ in (3–5 mm) long, maturing second year.

Principal uses: Bark is a source of tannin. Wood used locally for fuel, furniture, and mine timbers. Ornamental.

> *ee.* Leaves with side veins not parallel (except in No. 176), falling in autumn or evergreen; scales of acorn cup small and inconspicuous—**Oak** (Quercus).
>
> *f.* Leaves with bristle-tipped teeth; acorns maturing second year (first year in No. 174)—**Black oaks.**

173. California black oak, *Quercus kelloggii* Newb. (black oak, Kellogg oak). Large tree of Oregon and California. Bark dark brown, furrowed into irregular plates and ridges. Leaves falling in autumn, elliptic, 4–10 in (10–25 cm) long, usually 7-lobed about halfway to middle, each lobe with a few bristle-pointed teeth, thick, dark yellow green and hairless above, light yellow green and often hairy beneath. Acorns 1–1½ in (25–38 mm) long, rounded, with deep cup.
Principal use: Fuel.

174. Coast live oak, *Quercus agrifolia* Née (California live oak). Large tree of California and Lower California. Bark dark brown, thick, deeply furrowed. Leaves evergreen, elliptic to oblong, ¾–3 in (2–7.5 cm) long, short-pointed or rounded at tip, spiny-toothed, thick and stiff, dark green above, beneath paler, shiny, hairless or hairy. Acorns long, ¾–1½ in (20–38 mm) long, pointed, with deep cup.
Principal uses: Fuel. Shade tree and ornamental.

> *ff.* Leaves lobed, toothed, or entire but not bristle-tipped; acorns maturing first year (second year in No. 176)—**White oak** (see also Nos. 113 and 117).
>
> *g.* Leaves not lobed or only shallowly lobed.

175. Emory oak, *Quercus emoryi* Torr. (black oak, blackjack oak, bellota). Medium-sized tree of Southwestern region and adjacent Mexico. Bark blackish, divided into thin plates. Leaves evergreen, broadly lance-shaped, 1–2½ in (2.5–6 cm) long, short-pointed, with few short teeth, thick, stiff, leathery, flat, shiny dark green on both sides nearly hairless. Acorns ½–¾ in (12–30 mm) long, rounded, edible.
Principal uses: Fuel. Edible acorns (bellotas).

176. Canyon live oak, *Quercus chrysolepis* Liebm. (canyon oak, goldcup oak, live oak, maul oak, live white oak). Medium-sized to large tree of Pacific coast and Southwestern regions and adjacent Mexico. Bark gray brown, scaly and flaky. Leaves evergreen, elliptic or oval, 1–3 in (2.5–7.5 cm) long, with edges often spiny-toothed, thick and leathery, bright green and hairless above, yellow-hairy or whitish beneath. Acorns 1–2 in (25–50 mm) long, broad, with thick yellowish cup.
Principal uses: Parts of vehicles and agricultural implements. Ornamental. Fuel.

177. Blue Oak, *Quercus douglasii* Hook. & Arn. (California blue oak, mountain white oak, mountain oak, iron oak). Medium-sized tree of California. Bark gray, scaly. Leaves shedding in fall, oblong or elliptic, 1–3 in (2.5–7.5 cm) long, short-pointed or rounded at apex, with edges coarsely toothed, shallowly 4- or 5-lobed, or straight, rigid, pale blue green above, pale and slightly hairy beneath.
Principal use: Fuel.

> *gg.* Leaves deeply lobed halfway or more to middle.

178. Oregon white oak, *Quercus garryana* Dougl. (Garry oak, Oregon oak, post oak, white oak). Medium-sized to large tree of Pacific coast region from California to British Columbia (the only oak native in Washington). Bark light gray or brown, thin, with narrow fissures, broken into scaly ridges. Leaves shedding in fall, elliptic, 3–6 in (7.5–15 cm) long, deeply 5–9-lobed halfway or more to middle with blunt-pointed or slightly toothed lobes, dark green above, light green and usually hairy beneath. Acorns 1–1¼ in (25–30 mm) long, broad and rounded, with shallow cup.
Principal uses: Furniture, shipbuilding, construction, agricultural implements, cooperage, cabinetwork, interior finish, and fuel. Shade tree.

179. Valley oak, *Quercus lobata* Née (California white oak, valley white oak, white oak, water oak, weeping oak). Large tree of California. Bark gray or brown, thick, deeply furrowed and broken horizontally into thick plates. Leaves shedding in fall, elliptic, 2½–4 in (6–10 cm) long, broad, deeply 7–11-lobed more than halfway to middle, dark green above, gray-hairy beneath. Acorns long, 1¼–2¼ in (30–57 mm) long, slender and pointed, with deep cup.
Principal uses: Shade tree. Fuel.

180. Gambel oak, *Quercus gambelii* Nutt. (Rocky Mountain white oak, Utah white oak, white oak). Small tree or shrub of Rocky Mountain region, including adjacent Mexico.

| 177. Blue oak. | 178. Oregon white oak. | 179. Valley oak. | 180. Gambel oak. |

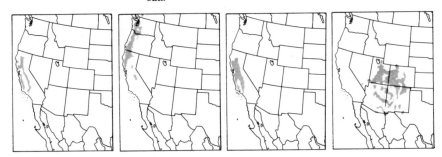

Bark gray brown, scaly. Leaves shedding in fall, elliptic, 4–8 in (10–20 cm) long, deeply 7–11-lobed halfway or more to middle, dark green above, light green and soft-hairy beneath. Acorns ⅝–¾ in (15–20 mm) long, broad and rounded, with deep cup.
Principal uses: Fenceposts and fuel.

HAWAII

Tree species Nos. 181–192 are 12 of the most common species of the native and introduced tropical forest trees. Also, the following and perhaps others in this handbook are introduced in Hawaii: Nos. 5, 6, 26, 50, 130, 147, 153.

DICOTYLEDONS (BROADLEAF TREES OR HARDWOODS)

A. Leaves reduced to minute scales on wiry jointed drooping green twigs—181.

181. Casuarina, *Casuarina equisetifolia* J. R. & G. Forst. (horsetail casuarina, beefwood, Australian beefwood, "shortleaf ironwood," "false ironwood," "Australian-pine;" "pino australiano," Puerto Rico and Spanish). Medium-sized evergreen tree common along sandy coasts and lowlands, planted and naturalized. Native of tropical Asia and Australia but planted and naturalized in tropics and subtropics, including Marianas Islands, southern Florida, Puerto Rico, and Virgin Islands. Bark light gray brown, becoming rough, furrowed, and shaggy. Twigs wiry, dropping, dark green, needlelike, about ¹⁄₃₂ in (1 mm) in diameter, jointed, with rings of minute scale leaves. Flowers numerous small, in light brown clusters, male narrow and terminal, female rounded and lateral. Fruit a light brown warty conelike ball ½–¾ in (12–20 mm) in diameter, with many winged seeds.
Principal uses: Windbreak, shade, ornament, erosion control. Bark has been used in tanning.

AA. Leaves mostly broad, green.
  B. Leaves and usually branches in pairs (opposite).
    C. Fruit egg-shaped, 1-seeded; flowers small—182.

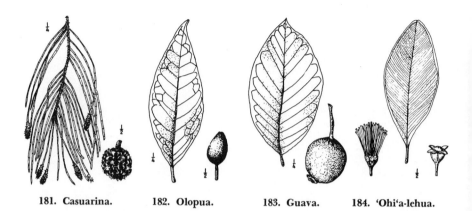

181. Casuarina.   182. Olopua.   183. Guava.   184. 'Ohi'a-lehua.

182. Olopua, pua, *Osmanthus sandwicensis* (Gray) Knobl. Medium-sized evergreen tree common in dry forests mainly at 600–4,000 ft (180–1,200 m) altitude, especially on leeward sides of all islands of Hawaii. Bark gray, thick, rough, much fissured. Leaves paired, mostly oblong, variable in size, 3–6 in (7.5–15 cm) long, leathery, dark green, hairless short-stalked. Flowers small, less than ¼ in (6 mm) long, pale yellow, 4-lobed, several at leaf bases. Fruit egg-shaped ½–⅞ in (12–22 mm) long, blue black, slightly fleshy to dry, the large stone 1-seeded.

Principal use: Formerly by Hawaiians for tool handles.

    CC. Fruit otherwise, many-seeded; flowers large with many threadlike stamens—**Myrtle family** (Myrtaceae), Nos. 183–185.

183. Guava, *Psidium guajava* L. (common guava; guayaba, Puerto Rico and Spanish). Small evergreen tree or weedy shrub, common in thickets, lowlands to about 3,500 ft (1,070 m) altitude. Native of tropical America, widely planted and naturalized through the tropics including Hawaii, Guam, southern Florida, Puerto Rico, and Virgin Islands. Bark smooth brown, scaling off in thin sheets, exposing green beneath. Leaves paired, oblong or elliptic, 2–5 in (5–13 cm) long, short-pointed or rounded at both ends, light green, hairy beneath, very short-stalked. Flowers few at leaf bases, large, white, about 1½ in (4 cm) across the 4–5 spreading petals. Fruit a yellow round or pear-shaped berry 1¼–2½ in (3–6 cm) in diameter, with many seeds in juicy, pinkish or yellow pulp, sweet or sour, edible.

Principal uses: Cultivated fruit tree, the edible fruits also prepared into juice, paste, and jelly. Charcoal.

184. 'Ohi'a-lehua, *Metrosideros collina* (Forst.) Gray (ssp. *polymorpha* (Gaud.) Rock; ohia, lehua). Large evergreen tree, sometimes shrub, the most abundant and widespread throughout Hawaii, of largest size in wet forests, 1,000–9,000 ft (300–2,700 m) altitude, very variable. Bark gray, rough, scaly. Trunks often consist of compacted stiltlike air roots. Leaves crowded, paired, small, oblong, ovate, or rounded, 1–3 in (2.5–7.5 cm) long, shiny, stiff, thick, often hairy, mostly short-stalked. Flowers in terminal showy red clusters, or pink, salmon, yellow, or white, formed by a mass of many long threadlike stamens about 1¼ in (3 cm) broad. Fruit a small capsule ¼ in (6 mm) long with many minute seeds.

Principal uses: Flooring, ship blocking, pallets, veneer, decorative poles. A honey plant. (Official county flower of island of Hawaii.)

    BB. Leaves and usually branches borne singly (alternate).
      D. Leaves not divided into leaflets (simple).
        E. Leaves narrow, not lobed—Nos. 185, 186 (see also No. 192).

185. Robusta eucalyptus, *Eucalyptus robusta* J. E. Smith (swamp-mahogany eucalyptus, beakpod eucalyptus; eucalipto, Puerto Rico and Spanish). Large evergreen tree common in forest plantations on the five main Hawaiian islands to 3,500 ft (1,050 m) in moist locations. Native of Australia but introduced into many tropical and subtropical areas including southern Florida and Puerto Rico. Bark thick, reddish brown, deeply furrowed, sometimes with grayish surface, fibrous, and very soft. Leaves alternate, broadly lance-shaped, 4–8 in (10–20 cm) long, slightly curved, long-pointed, leathery, aromatic, short-stalked.

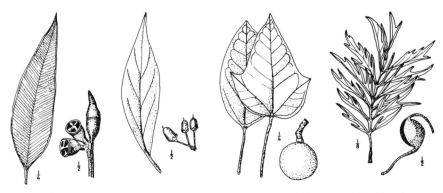

185. Robusta eu-   186. Naio, false san-   187. Kukui, candle-   188. Silk-oak.
    calyptus.   dalwood.   nut.

Flowers several on flattened stalk at leaf bases, cream-colored, 1¼ in (3 cm) across very many threadlike stamens. Fruit a cuplike dark green, seed capsule ½–⅝ in (12–15 mm) long, with many minute seeds.

Principal uses: Pallets, house siding, flooring, paneling, plywood, furniture, posts. Shade tree. A honey plant.

186. Naio, false sandalwood, *Myoporum sandwicense* Gray (aaka). Small to large evergreen tree, sometimes shrub, common in dry forest, also in wet forest, widely distributed from sea level to 10,000 ft (3,000 m) altitude, all islands of Hawaii. Bark gray, rough, irregularly furrowed. Leaves crowded, narrowly elliptic or lance-shaped, 2½–6 in (6–15 cm) long, pointed at both ends, shiny, short-stalked. Flowers clustered at leaf bases, 5-parted, bell-shaped, ⅜ in (1 cm) wide, white to pink. Fruit oblong or rounded, ¼ in (6 mm) long, whitish, fleshy or dry.

Principal uses: Formerly used for house timbers and as a substitute for sandalwood.

    EE. Leaves about as broad as long, often 3–5-lobed—187.

187. Kukui, candlenut, *Aleurites moluccana* (L.) Willd. (candlenut-tree, Indian-walnut; nuez, Puerto Rico). Medium-sized to large evergreen tree, recognized by the whitish foliage, common on lower mountain slopes and in valleys from sea level to 2,200 ft (670 m) altitude, apparently introduced by the original Polynesian inhabitants. Native probably of Malay region and west Polynesia, the original home uncertain, and introduced elsewhere through the tropics; uncommon in Guam, Puerto Rico, and Virgin Islands. Bark gray brown, smoothish with many fine fissures. Leaves variable, mostly ovate and with 3–5 main veins and lobes, 4–8 in (10–20 cm) long and broad, hairy, long-stalked. Flowers many, small, whitish, male and female, ⅜ in (1 cm) long, in same large terminal clusters. Fruit rounded, brown, 1½–2 in (4–5 cm) in diameter, fleshy, containing 1–2 large elliptic nutlike, hard oily seeds.

Principal uses: Nuts poisonous and medicinal (when roasted, sometimes eaten in very small quantities but purgative), the oil formerly exported for paints and varnishes and medicine. Shade and ornament. State tree of Hawaii, selected because of its many uses by the ancient Hawaiians for light, fuel, medicine, dye, ornaments, and beauty.

    D. Leaves divided into leaflets (compound).
      F. Leaves fernlike, leaflets deeply divided into narrow pointed lobes—188.

188. Silk-oak, *Grevillea robusta* A. Cunn. (silver-oak; roble de seda, Puerto Rico). Large tree, deciduous or partly so, planted and naturalized from sea level to 4,000 ft (1,200 m) altitude. Native of Australia but planted and naturalized in tropical and subtropical regions including Hawaii and southern Florida; planted but uncommon in southern California, southern Arizona, Puerto Rico, and Guam. Bark gray, smooth, becoming rough with many deep furrows. Leaves fernlike, compound, 6–12 in (15–30 cm) long, with many paired leaflets, above dark green, beneath with silky whitish or ash-colored hairs. Flowers showy, yellowish, ½ in (12 mm) long, crowded on 1 side of axis. Fruit black, curved pod-like, ¾ in (2 cm) long, with 1–2 winged seeds.

Principal uses: Furniture, turnery, paneling, face veneer (elsewhere). Fuel, shade, ornament. A honey plant.

      FF. Leaves otherwise, leaflets not divided or lobed—**Legume family** (Leguminosae),
        Nos. 189–192.

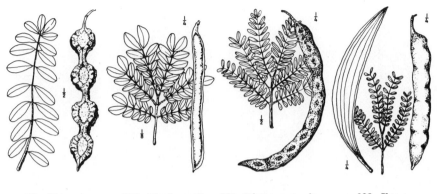

189. Mamane.   190. Monkeypod.   191. Kiawe, mesquite.   192. Koa.

189. Mamane, *Sophora chrysophylla* (Salisb.) Seem. Small to medium-sized evergreen tree, sometimes a shrub, all islands of Hawaii except Molokai, mainly in dry, mountain forests, at 4,000–8,000 ft (1,200–2,400 m) altitude. Bark gray brown, rough, furrowed into scaly ridges. Leaves compound, 5–6 in (12.5–15 cm) long, with 12–20 paired oblong blunt leaflets ¾–1¼ in (2–3 cm) long, mostly silvery gray, hairy beneath. Flowers beanlike, golden yellow, ½–1 in (12–25 mm) long, several in unbranched clusters. Fruit a pod 4–6 in (10–15 cm) long and more than ¼ in (6 mm) wide, 4-winged, deeply narrowed between the 4–8 oval beanlike yellow seeds.

Principal uses: Fence posts, formerly tool handles, forage for livestock. On Mauna Kea an important food source for the endangered endemic palilo bird.

190. Monkeypod, *Pithecellobium saman* (Jacq.) Benth. (raintree; samán, Puerto Rico and Spanish; *Samanea saman* (Jacq.) Merrill). Large, widely spreading evergreen tree native from Mexico to Brazil and Peru. Widely planted and naturalized through the tropics including coastal areas of Hawaii, Guam, Puerto Rico, and Virgin Islands; introduced in Southern Florida. Bark gray, rough furrowed into plates or ridges. Leaves 10–16 in. (25–40 cm) long, twice divided (compound), with many paired diamond-shaped leaflets ¾–1½ in (2–4 cm) long on 2–6 pairs of axes. Flowers many in heads 2½ in (6 cm) across, pinkish, tinged with green, with many spreading threadlike pinkish stamens. Fruit a flattened brown or blackish pod 4–8 in (10–20 cm) long and ⅝–¾ in (15–20 mm) wide, with sweetish pulp.

Principal uses: Shade and ornament. Carved bowls, craftwood, furniture, paneling, cabinetwork, seed leis.

191. Kiawe, mesquite, *Prosopis pallida* (Humb. & Bonpl. ex Willd.) H.B.K. (algarroba, Puerto Rico and Spanish). Small to medium-sized deciduous tree or shrub, widely naturalized and common in Hawaii's dry lowlands. Native of Peru and Ecuador, introduced in 1828; naturalized in Puerto Rico and Virgin Islands. Bark gray brown, smoothish becoming furrowed on angled trunks; twigs often with single or paired spines. Leaves about 2 in (5 cm) long, twice divided (compound), with many narrow paired leaflets ½–1 in (12–25 mm) long on 2–3 pairs of axes. Flowers many, less than ¼ in (6 mm) long, greenish yellow, crowded along an axis. Fruit a narrow yellowish pod 4–8 in (10–20 cm) long and ⅜ in (1 cm) wide with spongy sweetish pulp and several beanlike seeds in 4-angled cases.

Principal uses: Fenceposts, fuelwood, and charcoal. Pods and foliage are eaten by livestock. Shade for livestock. A honey plant.

192. Koa, *Acadia koa* Gray. Large evergreen tree, the largest in Hawaii and second most common, both in dry forests and rain forests at 600–7,000 ft (180–2,100 m) altitude. Bark gray, smooth to rough, scaly, thick. Leaves mostly modified as flattened, sickle-shaped green or yellow-green leathery leafstalks (phyllodes) 4–6 in (10–15 cm) long and ¼–1 in (6–25 mm) wide. True (juvenile) leaves on seedlings and young twigs twice divided (compound), 6–7 in (15–18 cm) long, with 5–7 paired axes, each with 24–30 paired stalkless oblong leaflets ¼ in (6 mm) long. Flowers many, pale yellow, crowded in balls ⅜ in (1 cm) in diameter. Fruit a brown flat, straight pod 3–6 in (7.5–15 cm) long, mostly not splitting open, with several beanlike seeds.

Principal uses: Furniture, cabinetwork, carved bowls and turnery, gunstocks, veneer. Formerly used for surfboards. Important habitat for rare birds.

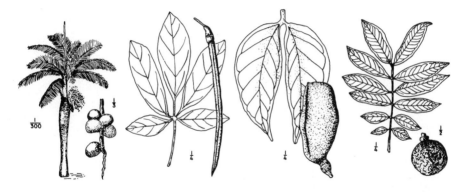

193. **Palma real,**   194. **Roble blanco.**   195. **Algarrobo, West-**   196. **Guaraguao,**
      Puerto Rico   **Indian-locust.**   **American**
      royalpalm.   **muskwood.**

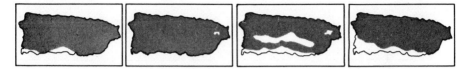

PUERTO RICO AND THE VIRGIN ISLANDS

Tree species Nos. 193–204 are 12 of the most common of more than 550 species of native tropical forest trees. Also, No. 26 is native and the following and perhaps others of this handbook are introduced: Nos. 50, 181, 183, 185, 187, 188, 190, 191. No. 197 is native also in southern Florida and No. 200 in southeastern continental United States. Nos. 194, 195, 196, 199, 201, and 202 are planted in southern Florida.

MONOCOTYLEDONS

A. Leaves parallel-veined, evergreen, clustered at top of trunk; trunk with woody portions irregularly distributed, without clear distinction of bark and wood, and without annual rings—**Monocotyledons** (palms, etc.).

193. Palma real, Puerto Rico royalpalm, *Roystonea borinquena* O. F. Cook. Large robust palm common almost throughout Puerto Rico except upper mountains and dry valleys; Vieques and St. Croix. Trunk gray, smoothish, stout, slightly enlarged at some distance above base. Leaves very large, compound (pinnate), with sheaths in light green narrow column 4 ft (1.2 m) high and blade 8–12 ft (2.4–3.7 m) long composed of many narrow paired leathery segments, green with parallel veins. Flowers small whitish, male and female, 3-parted, in large slightly drooping clusters below the eaves. Fruits many, light brown, elliptic, $\frac{1}{2}$ in (12 mm) long, slightly fleshy, 1-seeded.

Principal uses: Ornamental, honey plant. Rural construction and thatch.

DICOTYLEDONS (BROADLEAF TREES OR HARDWOODS)

AA. Leaves net-veined; trunk with bark and wood distinct and with annual rings in wood except in tropics—**Dicotyledons** (broadleaf trees or hardwoods).

B. Leaves and usually branches in pairs (opposite)—194.

194. Roble blanco, "white-cedar," *Tabebuia heterophylla* (DC.) Britton. Small to medium-sized, mostly deciduous tree common throughout Puerto Rico except upper mountains and through Virgin Islands; Hispaniola and Lesser Antilles; naturalized in Bermuda and planted in southern Florida. Bark rough and furrowed, gray to brown. Leaves paired, compound (palmate), 6–12 in (15–30 cm) long, with 5 or fewer (sometimes only 1) unequal elliptic or reverse lance-shaped leaflets 2–6 in (5–15 cm) long, blunt-pointed, slightly thickened, hairless except for dotlike scales, above slightly shiny green, paler beneath. Flowers in

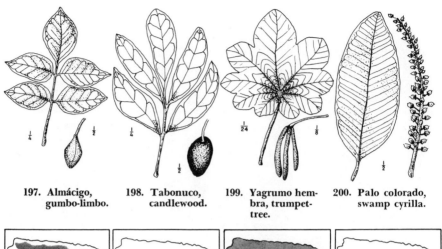

| 197. Almácigo,
gumbo-limbo. | 198. Tabonuco,
candlewood. | 199. Yagrumo hem-
bra, trumpet-
tree. | 200. Palo colorado,
swamp cyrilla. |

showy masses covering tree in spring, pink tubular funnel-shaped, 5-lobed, 2–3½ in (5–9 cm) long. Fruits dark brown cigarlike pods 3–8 in (7.5–20 cm) long, with numerous thin 2-winged seeds.

Principal uses: Construction, posts and poles, furniture, cabinetwork. Ornament, shade, honey plant.

   BB. Leaves and usually branches borne singly (alternate, sometimes crowded).
     C. Leaves divided into leaflets (compound), mostly attached along the extended leaf-stalk (pinnate).
      D. Leaflets all paired, 2 or 8–20 (even pinnate).

195. Algarrobo, West-Indian-locust, courbaril, *Hymenaea courbaril* L. Large, usually evergreen tree of moist and dry coastal and limestone regions of Puerto Rico and Virgin Islands; through West Indies and central Mexico to Brazil and Peru; rarely planted in southern Florida. Bark smoothish gray. Leaves with 2 almost stalkless, very unequal-sided, oblong, pointed, shiny green leaflets 2–4 in (5–10 cm) long, hairless, slightly thickened. Flowers numerous in erect clusters, whitish, 1¼ in (3 cm) wide, with 5 petals. Fruit an erect large oblong thick, dark brown pod 2–4 in (5–10 cm) long, with few dark red seeds in pale yellow pulp, edible but malodorous.

Principal uses: Furniture, carpentry, construction. Resinlike gum from roots and trunk has been used mainly in varnish. Shade and ornament, honey plant.

196. Guaraguao, American muskwood, *Guarea guidonia* (L.) Sleumer (*G. trichilioides* L.). Large evergreen tree of moist forests in Puerto Rico and St. Croix; Cuba, Hispaniola, and Costa Rica to Brazil and Argentina; introduced in southern Florida. Bark rough with many long fissures, reddish brown. Leaves large, compound (even pinnate), 8–24 in (20–60 cm) long, with 8–20 or more paired elliptic to oblong, glossy dark green leaflets 5–7 in (13–18 cm) long, short-pointed, forming new pairs of leaflets at tip. Flowers many, 4-parted greenish-white, ⅜–⅝ in (1–1.5 cm) wide, in long narrow branched clusters. Fruits reddish-brown capsules, nearly round, ⅝–¾ in (1.5–2 cm) in diameter, in grapelike clusters, 4-parted, with 4 or fewer reddish seeds.

Principal uses: Furniture, cabinetwork, construction, carpentry. Shade.

     DD. Leaflets paired except 1 at end, 5 or 7 (odd pinnate).

197. Almácigo, turpentine-tree, gumbo-limbo, *Bursera simaruba* (L.) Sarg. Medium-sized deciduous aromatic tree of coastal and lower mountain forests of Puerto Rico and Virgin Islands; southern Florida, through West Indies, and Mexico to Venezuela and Guyana. Bark smooth reddish brown or copper-colored, peeling off in paper flakes and exposing greenish brown layer beneath, exuding grayish resin with odor and taste like turpentine. Leaves compound (pinnate), 4–8 in (10–20 cm) long, with 5 or 7 oblong to ovate leaflets 1¼–3 in (3–7.5 cm) long, paired except at end, mostly hairless, green or dark green and

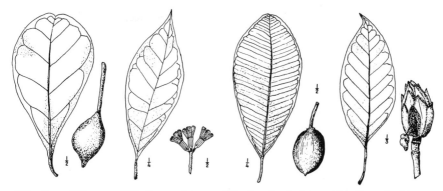

201. Granadillo.   **202. Capa prieto, onion cordia.**   **203. Ausubo, balata.**   **204. Laurel sabino.**

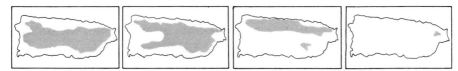

slightly shiny above, paler beneath. Flowers many small, whitish or yellowish green, 5-parted, about ³⁄₁₆ in (5 mm) across. Fruits diamond-shaped, slightly 3-angled, about ½ in (12 mm) long, dark pink, splitting into 3 parts, with usually 1 whitish seed.

Principal uses: Boxes and crates, cement forms, interior carpentry, light construction. The aromatic resin has served in medicine, glue, varnish, and incense. Living fenceposts and ornamental along highways.

198. Tabonuco, candlewood, *Dacryodes excelsa* Vahl. Very large evergreen, aromatic tree of lower mountain forests of Puerto Rico, formerly abundant, now restricted; Lesser Antilles. Bark smooth whitish, thin, peeling off in flakes, exuding fragrant whitish resin from cuts; trunk slightly enlarged and sometimes buttressed at base. Leaves compound (pinnate), 6–10 in (15–25 cm) long, with 5 or 7 elliptic leaflets 2½–5 in (6–13 cm) long, paired except at end, short-pointed or rounded, slightly thickened, hairless, dark green, aromatic when crushed. Flowers small greenish, about ³⁄₁₆ in (5 mm) in much branched clusters, male and female on different trees. Fruit oblong, fleshy brown, 1 in (2.5 cm) long, 1-seeded.

Principal uses: Furniture, cabinetwork, interior trim, construction, carpentry, boxes. The resin formerly used for torches, incense, and calking boats.

    CC. Leaves not divided into leaflets (simple).
      E. Leaves few, very large, umbrellalike, with 7–11 large rounded lobes—199.

199. Yagrumo hembra, trumpet-tree, *Cecropia peltata* L. Medium-sized evergreen tree (deciduous in dry areas) abundant as a weed in open areas and forests throughout Puerto Rico and in Virgin Islands; throughout West Indies and from Southeastern Mexico to Guianas; planted as ornamental in Southern Florida. Trunk with smooth gray bark, rings or joints, and few stout high branches, sometimes with prop roots. Leaves few, alternate and clustered, very large, umbrellalike, 1–2½ ft (30–75 cm) across, composed of 7–11 large rounded lobes spreading at end of leafstalk almost as long, thick, above green, slightly rough, and hairless, beneath whitish or silvery and densely hairy. Flowers male (yellow) and female (gray) on different trees, minute, crowded in fingerlike hanging clusters. Fruits minute, in 2–5 fingerlike gray clusters 2½–4 in (6–10 cm) long.

Principal uses: Excelsior and insulation board (combined with cement), elsewhere boxes and crates, matchsticks, and paper pulp. Ornamental.

    EE. Leaves many, small or average, not lobed.

200. Palo colorado, swamp cyrilla, *Cyrilla racemiflora* L. Large evergreen tree common in upper mountain forests of Puerto Rico; Southeastern United States near coast from Virginia to Florida and Texas, planted north to New England; through West Indies, Mexico to Nicaragua, and Venezuela to northern Brazil. Bark reddish-brown, smoothish, thin, becoming whitish pink and spongy at base of large crooked, twisted trunks. Leaves lance-shaped to narrowly elliptic, 1½–3¼ in (4–8 cm) long, blunt, leathery, green and shiny, paler beneath, turning red before falling. Flowers many crowded, white, 5-parted, small, ⅛ in (3 mm) long in very narrow clusters. Fruits many small dry, egg-shaped, ⅛ in (3 mm) long, pink to red, with 2–3 seeds.

Principal uses: Furniture. Ornamental, honey plant.

201. Granadillo, *Buchenavia capitata* (Vahl) Eichl. Large deciduous tree of lower mountain, moist limestone, and moist coast forests of Puerto Rico; Tortola, through West Indies, Panama, and Venezuela to Brazil and Bolivia; planted in Southern Florida. Bark light brown, smoothish. Crown thin, with few spreading, nearly horizontal branches. Leaves crowded in erect clusters, reverse lance-shaped or spoon-shaped, small, 1½–3 in (4–7.5 cm) long, rounded at end, hairless or nearly so, shiny yellow green above, paler beneath. Flowers many small greenish, ⅛ in (3 mm) wide, clustered at end of short stalk. Fruit elliptic greenish ¾–⅞ in (20–22 mm) long, pointed, slightly fleshy, bitter, with 1 large stone.

Principal uses: Furniture, construction, cabinetwork, plywood, veneer. Shade tree, ornamental.

202. Capa prieto, onion cordia, *Cordia alliodora* (Ruiz & Pav.) Oken (capa). Medium-sized evergreen tree of moist limestone and lower mountain forests of Puerto Rico and Virgin Islands; through West Indies and central Mexico to Brazil and Peru; planted in Southern Florida. Bark gray or brown, fissured, becoming rough and thick. Branches in horizontal layers. Leaves elliptic or oblong, 2½–6 in (6–15 cm) long, pointed, slightly shiny yellow-green finely hairy beneath, with odor of garlic when crushed. Flowers crowded in large showy, erect clusters, white, tubular, 5-lobed, about ½ in (12 mm) long and broad, fragrant. Fruit a nutlet ¼ in (6 mm) long, oblong, 1-seeded, with brown calyx and corolla attached.

Principal uses: Furniture, cabinetwork, millwork, construction. Forest plantations, coffee shade, ornament; a honey plant.

203. Ausubo, balata, *Manilkara bidentata* (A. DC.) Chev. (bulletwood). Large evergreen tree of moist lowlands and lower mountain forests of Puerto Rico, also St. John and Tortola; Hispaniola, Lesser Antilles, Panama, and Venezuela to Brazil and Peru. Trunk with broad rounded buttresses, brown fissured scaly bark, and milky sap or latex. Leaves elliptic, 3½–10 in (9–25 cm) long, thick and leathery with edges slightly turned under, hairless, dark green above, and light green beneath. Flowers small whitish, about ¼ in (6 mm) long, several at base of leaf. Berry round or elliptic, 1–1¼ in (25–30 mm) long, with sweet sticky edible pulp and 1 shiny blackish seed.

Principal uses: Formerly the most important timber of Puerto Rico, used for construction; elsewhere, furniture, cabinetwork, crossties, utility poles, tool handles, flooring. Balata gum, made into novelties and souvenirs.

204. Laurel sabino, *Magnolia splendens* Urban. Large evergreen tree native only in upper Luquillo Mountains of Northeastern Puerto Rico. Bark gray, smoothish, slightly fissured, becoming rough. Leaves ovate or elliptic, 4–7 in (10–18 cm) long, pointed, thick, and leathery, above shiny dark green, beneath gray green with silky hairs. Flowers large, showy, fragrant, 3 in (7.5 cm) across the 6 or more white petals. Fruit conelike, 1½ in (4 cm) long, greenish, with many pods containing 2 red seeds.

Principal uses: Furniture, cabinetwork.

STATE TREES

Each of the 50 States has a State tree designated officially by law. Also the District of Columbia possesses an official tree. However, none has been selected by Puerto Rico or the Virgin Islands.

State trees have been added from the latest compilation (USDA, Forest Service 1972). The name of the State is inserted in parentheses after principal uses. A few species are honored by more than one State.

Information on State trees is condensed below. The tree species number follows the State name. A number in parentheses means that the law may not agree precisely with the scientific name used here. (Also the common name in the law may differ slightly.) In a few States, more than one species is involved, for example, oak or pine. In two, just a variety.

Several States have a native tree also as the State flower or floral emblem. Examples in this handbook, with tree species number, are: Arizona, 159; Connecticut, 64; Louisiana, 61; Maine, (3) "pine cone and tassel"; Mississippi, 61 (also State tree); North Carolina, 28; Pennsylvania, 64; Virginia, 28 (also State tree).

States which have adopted other native trees or treelike shrubs are: Hawaii, *Hibiscus;* Missouri, hawthorn (red haw, *Crataegus*); Nevada, sagebrush (*Artemisia*); New Mexico, *Yucca;* Washington, coast (Pacific) rhododendron (*Rhododendron macrophyllum*); West Virginia, big (rosebay) rhododendron (*Rhododendron maximum*). Four have selected fruit tree blossoms: Arkansas and Michigan, apple; Delaware, peach; and Florida, orange. The official flower of the U.S. Virgin Islands is a small tree, ginger-thomas (yellow-elder, *Tecoma stans*).

Alabama, (6)	Montana, 126
Alaska, 139	Nebraska, 73
Arizona, (160)	Nevada, 133
Arkansas, (9)	New Hampshire, 88
California, 147, 148	New Jersey, 99
Colorado, 138	New Mexico, 132
Connecticut, 120	New York, 29
Delaware, 70	North Carolina, (6)
District of Columbia, 100	North Dakota, 73
Florida, 25	Ohio, 39
Georgia, 112	Oklahoma, 65
Hawaii, 187	Oregon, 140
Idaho, 124	Pennsylvania, 18
Illinois, (99–120)	Rhode Island, 32
Indiana, 60	South Carolina, 25
Iowa, (99–120)	South Dakota, (16)
Kansas, (81)	Tennessee, 60
Kentucky, 60	Texas, 42
Louisiana, 1	Utah, 138
Maine, 3	Vermont, 29
Maryland, 120	Virginia, 28
Massachusetts, 73	Washington, 135
Michigan, 3	West Virginia, 29
Minnesota, 10	Wisconsin, 29
Mississippi, 61	Wyoming, (81)
Missouri, 28	

SELECTED REFERENCES

Native tree species outside the scope of this handbook can be found in larger publications and in others limited geographically, such as to one State. Selected references are arranged geographically below. Many other titles, including some for cultivated trees and for shrubs, are listed in the bibliography cited (Little and Honkala 1976).

General

Little, Elbert L., Jr.
1961. Sixty trees from foreign lands. U.S. Dep. Agric., Agric. Handb. 212, 30 p., illus.

Little, Elbert L., Jr.
1971. Atlas of United States trees, volume 1, conifers and important hardwoods. U.S. Dep. Agric. Misc. Publ. 1146, 9 p., illus. (313 maps, folio)

Little, Elbert L., Jr.
1978. Checklist of United States trees, native and naturalized. U.S. Dep. Agric., Agric. Handb. (In press.)

Little, Elbert L., Jr., and Barbara H. Honkala.

1976. Trees and shrubs of the United States: a bibliography for identification. U.S. Dep. Agric. Misc. Publ. 1336, 56 p.

Plank, Marlin E.
1971. Red alder (*Alnus rubra* Bong.). Revised. American Woods. U.S. Dep. Agric., For. Serv. FS–215, 7 p., illus. (First of a series of about 50 short publications on American Woods, mostly revised from an earlier series.)

U.S. Department of Agriculture, Forest Service.
1972. State trees. FS–63, rev. 4 p., illus. Washington, D.C.

Continental United States

Brockman, C. Frank.
1968. Trees of North America: a field guide to the major native and introduced species north of Mexico. Illustrated by Rebecca Merrilees. 280 p., illus. (col., maps). Golden Press, New York. (A Golden Field Guide.)

Collingwood, G. H., and Warren D. Brush.
1974. Knowing your trees: with more than 900 illustrations showing typical trees and their leaves, bark, flowers, and fruits. Rev. and ed. by Devereau Butcher. 374 p., illus. (maps). American Forestry Association, Washington, D.C.

Harlow, William M., and Ellwood S. Harrar.
1968. Textbook of dendrology: covering the important forest trees of the United States and Canada. 5th ed., 575 p., illus. (maps). McGraw-Hill Book Co., New York.

Miller, Howard A., and H. E. Jaques.
1972. How to know the trees. 2d ed., 302 p., illus. (maps). Wm. C. Brown, Dubuque. (Pictured-Key Nature Series.)

Preston, Richard Joseph, Jr.
1976. North American trees (exclusive of Mexico and tropical United States). 3d ed. 399 p., illus. (maps). Iowa State Univ. Press, Ames.

Sargent, Charles Sprague.
1965. Manual of the trees of North America (exclusive of Mexico). With 783 illustrations by Charles Edward Faxon and Mary W. Gill. 2d. corr. ed. 2 vol., 934 p., illus. Dover Publications, New York. (Reprint of 1926 revision, Houghton Mifflin and Co., Boston and New York. Also reprinted in 2 vol., 1962 by Peter Smith Publisher, Gloucester, Mass.)

Alaska

Viereck, Leslie A., and Elbert L. Little, Jr.
1972. Alaska trees and shrubs. U.S. Dep. Agric., Agric. Handb. 410, 265 p., illus. (maps).

Viereck, Leslie A., and Elbert L. Little, Jr.
1974. Guide to Alaska trees. U.S. Dep. Agric., Agric. Handb. 472, 98 p., illus. (maps).

Viereck, Leslie A., and Elbert L. Little, Jr.
1975. Atlas of United States trees, volume 2, Alaska trees and common shrubs. U.S. Dep. Agric. Misc. Publ. 1293, 19 p., illus. (105 maps).

Eastern

Coker, William Chambers, and Henry Roland Totten.
1945. Trees of the southeastern States including Virginia, North Carolina, South Carolina, Tennessee, Georgia, and northern Florida. 3d ed., 419 p., illus. Univ. N.C. Press, Chapel Hill. (Reprinted.)

Graves, Arthur Harmount.
1956. Illustrated guide to trees and shrubs: a handbook of the woody plants of the northeastern United States and adjacant regions. Rev. ed., 271 p., illus. Harper and Brothers, New York.

Grimm, William Carey.
1962. The book of trees. 2d ed., 487 p., illus. Stackpole Co., Harrisburg, Pa. (Revision of: The trees of Pennsylvania. 363 p., illus. 1950.)

Harlow, William M.
1957. Trees of the eastern and central United States and Canada. 288 p., illus. Dover Publications, New York. (Reprint of 1942 ed. McGraw Hill Book Co., New York.)

Harrar, Ellwood S., and J. George Harrar.
1962. Guide to southern trees. 2d ed., 709 p., illus. Dover Publications, New York. (The nomenclature has been revised.) (1st ed., 712 p., illus. McGraw-Hill Book Co., New York.)

Neelands, R. W., compil.
1973. Important trees of eastern forests. Illustrations by Rebecca Merrilees from Trees of North America by C. Frank Brockman (1968). 111 p., illus. (col., maps). U.S. Dep. Agric. For Serv., Region, Atlanta. [Unnumbered publ.]

Peattie, Donald Culross.
1966. Natural history of trees of eastern and central North America. With . . . 16 full-color photos by Herman A. Howard. Illustrated by Paul Landacre. 2d ed., 606 p., illus. (part col.). Houghton Mifflin Co., Boston.

Petrides, George A.
1972. A field guide to trees and shrubs: field marks of all trees, shrubs, and woody vines that grow wild in the north-eastern and north-central United States and in southeastern and south-central Canada. Illustrations by George A. Petrides, Roger Tory Peterson. 2d ed. 428 p., illus. (part col.). Houghton Mifflin Co., Boston. (The Peterson Field Guide Series: 11.)

Stephens, H. A.
1973. Woody plants of the North Central plains. 530 p., illus. (maps). Univ. Press Kans., Lawrence, Manhattan, Wichita.

Symonds, George W. D.
1958. The tree identification book. 372 p., illus. William Morrow & Co., New York.

Western

Baerg, Harry J.
1973. How to know the western trees. 2d ed., 179 p., illus. (maps). Wm. C. Brown Co., Dubuque, Iowa. (Pictured Key Nature Series.)

Benson, Lyman, and Robert A. Darrow.
1954. The trees and shrubs of the southwestern deserts. Line drawings by Lucretia Breazeale Hamilton. 2d ed., 437 p., illus. (part col., maps). Univ. Ariz. Press, Tucson, and Univ. N. Mex. Press, Albuquerque.

Berry, James Berthold.
1966. Western forest trees: a guide to the identification of trees and woods for students, teachers, farmers and woodsmen. Illustrated from photographs and with drawings by Mary E. Eaton. Corrected and reprinted. 251 p., illus. Dover Publications, New York. (First published: 1924. 212 p., illus. World Book Co., Yonkers-on-Hudson, N.Y.)

Little, Elbert L., Jr.
1950. Southwestern trees: a guide to the native species of New Mexico and Arizona. U.S. Dep. Agric., Agric. Handb. 9, 109 p., illus.

McMinn, Howard E., and Evelyn Maino.
   1946. An illustrated manual of Pacific
   Coast trees. 2d ed., 409 p., illus.
   Univ. of Calif. Press, Berkeley. (Reprinted 1956. 1st ed. 1935. 409 p.,
   illus.)
Peattie, Donald Culross.
   1953. A natural history of western trees,
   illustrated by Paul Landacre. 715 p.
   illus. Houghton Mifflin Co., Boston.
Preston, Richard J., Jr.
   1968. Rocky Mountain trees: a handbook
   of native species with plates and distribution maps. 3d rev. ed., 285 p.,
   illus. (maps). Dover Publications,
   New York.

Sudworth, George B.
   1967. Forest trees of the Pacific Slope.
   With a new foreword by Woodbridge
   Metcalf and a new table of changes in
   nomenclature by E. S. Harrar. 455
   p., illus. Dover Publications, New
   York. (First published: 1908. 441
   p., illus. U.S. Dep. Agric. For. Serv.,
   Washington, D.C. [unnumbered
   publ.].)
Vines, Robert A.
   1960. Trees, shrubs and woody vines of
   the southwest. With drawings by
   Sarah Kahlden Arendole. 1,104 p.,
   illus. Univ. Tex. Press, Austin.

Hawaii

Little, Elbert L., Jr., and Roger E. Skolmen.
   1979. Common forest trees of Hawaii.
   U.S. Dep. Agric., Agric Handb. (In
   press.)
Rock, Joseph F.
   1974. The indigenous trees of the Ha-

waiian Islands. 2d ed., 548 p., illus.
Charles E. Tuttle Co., Rutland, Vt.,
and Tokyo, Japan. (Reprint of 1913
ed. with updated nomenclature by
Derral Herbst and an introduction by
Sherwin Carlquist.)

Puerto Rico and the Virgin Islands

Little, Elbert L., Jr., and Frank H. Wadsworth.
   1964. Common trees of Puerto Rico and
   the Virgin Islands. U.S. Dep. Agric.,
   Agric. Handb. 249, 548 p., illus.
   (maps).
Little, Elbert L., Jr., Frank H. Wadsworth,
   and José Marrero.
   1967. Arboles comunes de Puerto Rico
   y las Islas Vírgenes. 827 p., illus.

(part col.). Editorial, Universidad de
Puerto Rico, Rio Piedras, Puerto
Rico.
Little, Elbert L., Jr., Roy O. Woodbury, and
   Frank H. Wadsworth.
   1974. Trees of Puerto Rico and the Vir-
   gin Islands. Second volume. U.S.
   Dep. Agric., Agric. Handb. 449, 1,024
   p., illus.

INDEX OF COMMON NAMES

The numbers refer to species Nos. 1–204. In addition to these approved
common names, other common names in use are listed in the text.

INDEX OF SCIENTIFIC NAMES

The numbers refer to species Nos. 1–204. Widely used synonyms of these accepted scientific names are mentioned in the text.

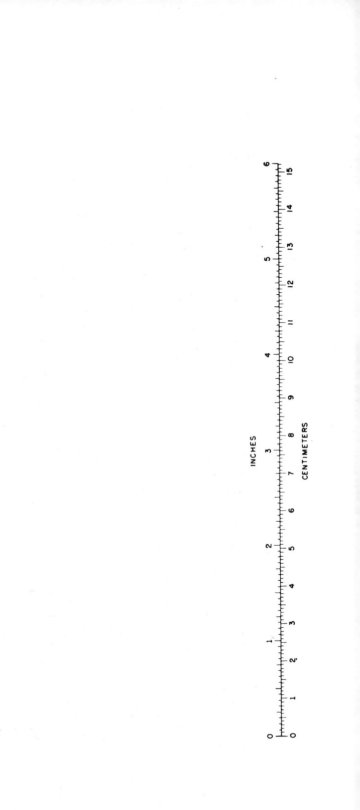